Making a Wedding Speech

JOHN BOWDEN

How to face the big occasion with confidence and carry it off with style

Every effort has been made to identify and acknowledge the sources of the material quoted throughout this book. The author and publishers apologise for any errors or omissions, and would be grateful to be notified of any corrections that should appear in any reprint or new edition.

Published by How To Books Ltd,
Spring Hill House, Spring Hill Road, Begbroke,
Oxford OX 5 1RX, United Kingdom
Tel: (01865) 375794. Fax: (01865) 379162
info@howtobooks.co.uk
www.howtobooks.co.uk

How To Books greatly reduce the carbon footprint of their books by sourcing their typesetting and printing in the UK.

Fifth edition 2000; Reprinted 2001 (twice); Reprinted 2002;
Reprinted 2003; Reprinted 2004; Reprinted 2006
Sixth edition published 2008

British Library Cataloguing in Publication Data
A catalogue record for this book is available from the British Library.

978 1 84528 294 3

Produced for How To Books by Deer Park Productions
Cover design by Baseline Arts Ltd, Oxford
Typeset by Kestrel Data, Exeter, Devon
Printed and bound by Cromwell Press, Trowbridge, Wiltshire

NOTE: The material contained in this book is set out in good faith for general guidance and no liability can be accepted for loss or expense incurred as a result of relying in particular circumstances on statements made in the book. Laws and regulations are complex and liable to change, and readers should check the current position with the relevant authorities before making personal arrangements.

Contents

Preface
to the Sixth Edition

So you have been asked 'to say a few words' on the big day. The problem is we don't get much practice, do we? That's why this book will prove so useful to you. It will show you how to prepare and deliver a unique and memorable little speech which even the most seasoned public speaker would be proud of. What's more, it's going to be fun!

Now in its sixth edition, this popular handbook is crammed with even more classics of humour and fresh one-liners that would prove surefire hits in any wedding speech. You'll find something old, something new, plenty borrowed, but absolutely nothing blue!

A speechmaker is a showman – a performer – an entertainer. That's why I am so indebted to the following funnymen and funnywomen who kindly took time out to tell me – and you – how they 'make 'em laugh':

Rowan Atkinson, Lenny Henry, Joanna Lumley, Leslie Phillips, Andrew Sachs, Mollie Sugden, Chris Tarrant and **Richard Wilson.**

For the first time you can study and apply the techniques and tricks of the trade that professional entertainers use to hold and captivate their audiences.

But enough about the menu, let's get to the meal. Bon appetit!

John Bowden

For Paula . . . forever

'Ladies and Gentlemen, this is only the second time I've ever been a best man. I hope I did the job alright last time. The couple in question are at least still talking to me. Unfortunately, they're not actually talking to each other . . . but I'm sure that has absolutely nothing to do with me. Apparently Paula knew Piers had slept with her younger sister before I mentioned it in my speech. The fact that he had slept with her mother came as a surprise.'

(Hugh Grant in *Four Weddings and a Funeral*)

1

Finding a Captivating Opening and Compelling Close

Think of your speech as a gourmet meal. Your opening lines should serve up a tasty little starter that really whets the audience's appetite for the main course. Your closing words should provide a delectable and memorable dessert with a delicious aftertaste.

There is no such thing as the *best* opening lines or the *best* closing lines for a speech, because every speech – and every speaker – is different. In this chapter you will learn a number of techniques that can be used to open and close a speech. They are all tried and tested, so you don't need to worry about choosing a dud. Study the options and decide what would work best for *your* speech – and for *you*.

There are dozens of ways to put over a great opening line or to deliver an emotionally charged big finish. It's just a matter of finding the pattern of words that suits your style and has exactly the effect you are after. Work on your lines until you've got them spot on. Then *memorise* them. You must know *precisely* how you arc going to open and close your speech. There is absolutely no room for any ad-libbing here.

GRABBING AN AUDIENCE'S ATTENTION

It is vital to have an opening line that really grabs your audience's attention. Entertainers call this having a hook. These are four of the best:

♦ hooking with humour

♦ hooking with a quotation

♦ hooking with anniversaries

♦ hooking with brackets.

The bride's father can begin his speech directly with one of these hooks, but the bridegroom and best man (and any other speakers) must remember to thank the previous speaker immediately before or soon after hooking their audience. However, to avoid repetition, I have included such thanks only with the first hook.

HOOKING WITH HUMOUR

Opening with a short and relevant joke or anecdote will help to relax you and get the audience laughing and even more on your side than they are already. Here are some possibilities:

Ladies and Gentlemen (thank you, Jim, for those kind words . . .), as Henry VIII said to each of his wives in turn, 'I shall not keep you long'.

Ladies and Gentlemen – the ladies is over there [*pointing*], and the gents is over there [*pointing*].

Ladies and Gentlemen, I must admit that I have made a very similar speech to this before. Once to the patients in Broadmoor, once to Aberdeen Naturalists' Group, and once to Penzance Haemorrhoid Sufferers Society – a stand-up buffet. So to those of you who have heard this speech three times already, I apologise.

Ladies and Gentlemen, Clive just asked me, 'Would you like to speak now, or should we let our guests enjoy themselves a little longer?'

Ladies and Gentlemen, the last time I made a wedding speech someone at the rear shouted, 'I can't hear you!' – and a man sitting next to me yelled back, 'I'll change places with you!'

Ladies and Gentlemen, the last time I made a wedding speech a man fell asleep. I asked a pageboy to wake him, and do you know what the little horror replied? He said, 'You wake him. You were the one who put him to sleep.'

Ladies and Gentlemen, before I start speaking I have something to say.

Ladies and Gentlemen. I feel like the young Arab Sheik who inherited his father's harem. I know exactly what to do, but where on earth do I begin?

Ladies and Gentlemen – well Brian did ask me to begin with a gag.

Ladies and Gentlemen – who says flattery doesn't pay?

Ladies and Gentlemen, what can I say about Stephen that hasn't already been said in open court?

Ladies and Gentlemen, this is the first time I've spoken at a wedding – except during other people's speeches.

Ladies and Gentlemen, since we must speak well of the dead, our only chance to knock them is while they're alive. So here goes . . .

Ladies and Gentlemen, my dad taught me always to remember the ABC and the XYZ of speechmaking. ABC: Always be concise. XYZ: Examine your zip [*look down*].

Ladies and Gentlemen, first the good news: when I saw Patrick's new suit/shirt/tie this morning I was absolutely speechless . . . Now the bad news: I've almost recovered from the shock, and the speech must go on.

Ladies and Gentlemen, Mary is the best daughter in the world – she's beautiful, charming, intelligent and, well, perfect in every way. She does everything for me – she even wrote this speech.

Ladies and Gentlemen, this is only the second time I've ever been a best man. I hope I did the job alright last time. The couple in question are at least still talking to me. Unfortunately, they're not actually talking to each other . . . but I'm sure that had absolutely nothing to do with me. Apparently Paula knew Piers had slept with her younger sister before I mentioned it in my speech. The fact that he slept with her mother came as a surprise. (Hugh Grant in *Four Weddings and a Funeral*). (If you use or adapt this opening, don't refer to a couple you really know!)

Ladies and Gentlemen, that speech put me in mind of a steer's horns. There was a sharp point here and a solid point there . . . but there was an awful lot of bull in between.

Ladies and Gentlemen, I'm sure you'll agree that you'll remember Nick's speech for the rest of your life. If you have a phenomenal memory . . . and have absolutely nothing else to think about . . . and you meet with a fatal accident on your way home.

Good ladies, afternoon and gentlemen . . . I *knew* I should have rehearsed this speech.

Ladies and Gentlemen, I won't take long. This suit has to be back in twenty minutes.

Ladies and Gentlemen, unaccustomed as I am to public speaking, I feel this irresistible urge to prove it.

Ladies and Gentlemen, just once in a lifetime you get the opportunity to talk about a man blessed with dynamic charisma, devastating wit, stupendous talent and unstoppable personality . . . but until the day comes along, I shall talk about Mark.

[*After a formal introduction by a toastmaster*] Ladies and Gentlemen, did he say pray *for* the silence of John Smith?

[*After being called upon to give an impromptu speech*] Ladies and Gentlemen, I am totally unprepared for this, but, as Big Ben said to the Leaning Tower of Pisa, 'I've got the time if you've got the inclination'.

Ladies and Gentlemen, my wife and I . . . (not a particularly funny hook but a very useful one for a bridegroom because it is guaranteed to raise howls of laughter, cheers and applause).

HOOKING WITH A QUOTATION

Here you simply begin your wedding speech with a short and relevant quotation. You will find plenty of these listed throughout Chapter 3. It is far safer to use a serious quote rather than a cynical one. Begin with something like this:

Ladies and Gentlemen, 'Love is a great force in life, it is indeed the greatest of all things.' So said E.M. Forster, and E.M. knew what he was talking about . . .

Ladies and Gentlemen, it has been said that 'marriages are made in heaven'. Well, I can tell you, this marriage was made in my sitting room . . .

Sometimes a quotation associated with the bride's or bridegroom's occupation can be adapted to make an excellent and original opening. For example, here are a couple of adaptations suitable for members of the armed services:

Ladies and Gentlemen, 'Some talk of Alexander, and some of Hercules, of Hector and Lysander and such great names as these.' But I would rather talk about Captain and Mrs Mainwaring.

Ladies and Gentlemen, 'When he was a lad he served a term. As an office boy to an Attorney's firm. He cleaned the windows and he swept the floor. And he polished up the handle of the big front door. He polished up that handle so carefullee. That now he's the Ruler of the Queen's Navee' – well, almost, anyway.

HOOKING WITH ANNIVERSARIES

Another wonderful way of grabbing an audience is to tell them that today is a truly historic day, not only because of the recent marriage but also because of other things that happened on this day in years gone by. It is best to mention two things as well as the marriage – probably a famous person's birth and some other memorable event.

As always, use your own words, but this is the sort of thing you should say:

Ladies and Gentlemen, this is a truly historic day! This day, the 18th of June, will always be remembered because of three earth-shattering events. Napoleon finally met his Waterloo at Waterloo in 1815, pop superstar Paul McCartney had his first day on earth in 1942, and on this day in 200X, Angus married Laura!

Ladies and Gentlemen, this is a day heavy with significance! This very day, the 1st of May, will always be associated with three of the most memorable events of the last hundred years. New York's Empire State Building opened in 1931, the Absolutely Fabulous Joanna Lumley was born in 1946, and on this day in 200X, Bernard married Lydia!

Get the idea? Below is a list of some famous blasts from the past. Simply look up the date of the wedding and you'll find an event and birth that also occurred on that day in years gone by. If they don't seem quite right for your speech, take a look at one or two of the specialist anniversary books listed on page 211.

January

1 1877 Queen Victoria was proclaimed Empress of India. 1919 Writer J.D. Salinger was born.
2 1920 Sci-fi writer Isaac Asimov was born. 1967 Dr Christian Bernard performed the first heart transplant operation.
3 1924 British archaeologist Howard Carter discovered Tutankhamen's tomb. 1956 Actor Mel Gibson was born.
4 1785 Fairy tale writer Jacob Grimm was born. 1982 Erica Rowe streaked to fame at Twickenham.
5 1933 The construction of California's Golden Gate Bridge began. 1946 Actress Diane Keaton was born.
6 1838 Samuel Morse demonstrated his electric telegraph system for the first time. 1960 Domestic goddess Nigella Lawson was born.
7 1785 Parachute-inventing Jean-Pierre Blanchard made the first balloon crossing of the Channel. 1951 *Coronation Street*'s Gail Platt (alias actress Helen Worth) was born.
8 1921 Chequers became the official residence of British Prime Ministers. 1935 The King, Elvis Presley was born.
9 1799 Income tax was introduced in Britain as a so-called

temporary measure. 1965 Actress Joely Richardson was born.

10 1840 Rowland Hill's Penny Post was introduced in Britain. 1945 Rocker Rod Stewart was born.

11 1569 Tickets went on sale for Britain's first ever National Lottery. 1963 Actor Jason Connery was born.

12 1951 Actress Kirstie Alley was born. 1970 The first jumbo jet transatlantic flight was made.

13 1961 Singer Graham 'Suggs' McPherson was born. 1989 Computers were hit by the 'Friday the 13th' virus.

14 1878 Queen Victoria made Britain's first phone call. 1941 Oscar-winning actress Faye Dunaway was born.

15 1559 Elizabeth I began her 44 year reign. 1926 Rock legend Chuck Berry was born.

16 1920 The prohibition era began in America. 1974 Style icon Kate Moss was born.

17 1962 Actor/comedian Jim Carey was born. 1983 Breakfast television began in Britain.

18 1788 Captain Cook discovered Hawaii. 1955 Actor Kevin Costner was born.

19 1903 Competitors were invited to take part in the first Tour de France cycle race. 1946 Singer Dolly Parton was born.

20 1850 It rained stones in Italy and Warsaw experienced a shower of caterpillars. 1971 Singer Gary Barlow was born.

21 1940 Golf legend Jack Nicklaus was born. 1976 Concorde made its first commercial flight.

22 1902 Marconi made his first radio transmission. 1941 Opera superstar Placido Domingo was born.

23 1899 Screen legend Humphrey Bogart was born. 1985 House of Lords debates were first televised.

24 1941 Singer Neil Diamond was born. 1848 The Californian Gold Rush began.

25 1327 King Edward III was crowned. 1882 Novelist Virginia Woolf was born.

26 1828 The Duke of Wellington became Prime Minister. 1925 Oscar-winning actor Paul Newman was born.

27 1832 Author/mathematician Lewis Carroll was born. 1926 John Logie Baird switched on the world's first television.

28 1788 The first Australian penal colony was founded at Botany Bay. 1957 Funnyman Frank Skinner was born.

29 1856 The Victoria Cross was instituted. 1945 Actor Tom Selleck was born.

30 1649 Charles I lost his head in London. 1931 Actor Gene Hackman was born.

31 1969 The Beatles gave their final live performance. 1981 Singer/actor Justin Timberlake was born.

February

1 1901 Screen legend Clark Gable was born. 1940 Captain Marvel made his debut in *Whiz Comics.*

2 1709 Alexander Selkirk – the real Robinson Crusoe – was rescued after five years on a desert island. 1940 Del Boy (alias actor David Jason) was born.

3 1874 U.S. writer Gertrude Stein was born. 1966 Russia's *Luna 9* landed on the moon.

4 1926 Malcolm Campbell broke the world land speed record. 1948 Rocker Alice Cooper was born.

5 1946 Actress Charlotte Rampling was born. 1989 Sky TV was launched.

6 1945 Reggae legend Bob Marley was born. 1952 Elizabeth II succeeded to the throne.

7 1812 Victorian novelist Charles Dickens was born. 1964

The Beatles arrived in America and took the country by storm.

8 1931 Cult hero James Dean was born. 1974 Skylab space station astronauts returned safely to Earth after 85 days in space.

9 1891 Screen legend Ronald Colman was born. 1983 Derby winning racehorse Shergar disappeared.

10 1940 Singer Roberta Flack was born. 1942 Glenn Miller was presented with the first-ever gold disc – for *Chattanooga Choo Choo.*

11 1972 Singer Sheryl Crow was born. 1990 Nelson Mandela made his long march to freedom after 26 years' imprisonment.

12 1688 England's 'Glorious Revolution' began. 1809 Scientist Charles Darwin was born.

13 1692 The Macdonalds were massacred by the Campbells at Glencoe. 1944 Talk show host Jerry Springer sprang into the world.

14 1929 The St Valentine's Day Massacre took place in Chicago. 1946 Singer Gregory Hines was born.

15 1951 Actress Jane Seymour was born. 1971 Decimal currency was introduced in Britain.

16 1923 Howard Carter opened Tutankhamen's tomb. 1959 Tennis ace John McEnroe was born.

17 1863 The International Red Cross was founded in Geneva. 1934 Housewife megastar Dame Edna Everage was born in Wagga-Wagga.

18 1954 American actor John Travolta was born. 1979 Snow fell in the Sahara Desert for the first and only time.

19 1924 Screen bad guy Lee Marvin was born. 1985 The first episode of *Eastenders* was broadcast.

20   1962 John Glenn became the first US astronaut to orbit the Earth. 1988 R&B singer Rihanna was born.

21   1986 Singer Charlotte Church was born. 2004 Derek the Sheep made his debut in the *Beano*.

22   1797 The last invasion of Britain was attempted (by the French at Fishguard). 1974 Singer/songwriter James Blunt was born.

23   1685 Composer George Frederic Handel was born. 1836 The siege of the Alamo began.

24   1920 Nancy Astor became the first woman MP to speak in the House of Commons. 1940 Soccer legend Denis Law was born.

25   1943 Guitarist George Harrison was born. 1964 Muhammad Ali became world heavyweight boxing champion.

26   1815 Napoleon escaped from Elba. 1932 Singer Johnny Cash was born.

27   1932 Screen legend Liz Taylor was born. 1991 The Gulf War ended.

28   1957 TV chef Ainsley Harriott was born. 1983 A record 125 million American viewers watched the final episode of *M*A*S*H*.

29   1904 Big band leader Jimmy Dorsey was born. 2008 Prince Harry was ordered home after his front line duties in Afghanistan were revealed on the internet.

March

1   1555 Nostradamus's book of predictions was published. 1944 Rock singer Roger Daltrey was born.

2   1969 Concorde made its maiden flight. 1977 Coldplay's frontman Chris Martin was born.

3   1847 Inventor Alexander Graham Bell was born. 2005

Steve Fossett became the first man to fly an aeroplane around the world, solo without any stops or refuelling.

4 1678 Composer Antonio Vivaldi was born. 1975 Charlie Chaplin received his knighthood from the Queen.

5 1946 Sir Winston Churchill made his famous 'Iron Curtain' speech. 1952 Singer Elaine Page was born.

6 1475 Renaissance painter Michelangelo was born. 1836 The Alamo fell.

7 1875 Composer Maurice Ravel was born. 1933 The board game Monopoly was first put on the market.

8 1917 The Russian Revolution began. 1943 Actress Lynn Redgrave was born.

9 1796 Napoleon married Josephine. 1918 Crime writer Mickey Spillane was born.

10 1801 Britain's first census was carried out. 1964 Singer/ songwriter Neneh Cherry was born.

11 1952 *Hitchhikers' Guide to the Galaxy* creator Douglas Adams was born. 1985 Mikhail Gorbachev became leader of the USSR.

12 1918 Moscow became the capital of Russia. 1946 Singer/ actress Liza Minnelli was born.

13 1781 William Herschel discovered Uranus. 1939 Singer/ songwriter Neil Sedaka was born.

14 1794 Eli Whitney was granted patent on the cotton gin. 1933 Actor Michael Caine was born (not a lot of people know that).

15 44 BC Julius Caesar was assassinated. 1946 Crime writer Lynda La Plante was born.

16 1872 Wanderers became the first FA Cup winners. 1926 Funnyman Jerry Lewis was born.

17 1964 Actor Rob Lowe was born. 1973 Pink Floyd released their classic album *Dark Side of the Moon.*

18 1941 Soul legend Wilson Pickett was born. 1965 Cosmonaut Aleksey Leonov made the first space walk.

19 1932 Sydney Harbour Bridge was opened. 1947 Actress Glenn Close was born.

20 1917 Singer Dame Vera Lynn was born. 1969 John Lennon married Yoko Ono.

21 1946 Actor Timothy Dalton was born. 1963 Alcatraz prison was closed.

22 1888 The English Football League was founded. 1943 Singer George Benson was born.

23 1848 The first settlers landed in New Zealand. 1904 Screen legend Joan Crawford was born.

24 1930 Actor Steve McQueen was born. 1998 *Titanic* steamed to a record-equalling 11 Oscars.

25 1947 Pop superstar Elton John was born. 1957 The Common Market was set up.

26 1944 Superstar Diana Ross was born. 2006 Smoking in public places was banned in Scotland.

27 1942 Actor Michael York was born. 1989 The first democratic election for the Russian parliament took place.

28 1921 Actor Dirk Bogarde was born. 1939 The Spanish Civil War ended.

29 1871 London's Albert Hall opened. 1943 Funnyman Eric Idle was born.

30 1867 The USA bought Alaska from Russia. 1945 Guitar legend Eric Clapton was born.

31 1889 The Eiffel Tower was opened. 1943 Actor Christopher Walken was born.

April

1 1918 The RAF was founded. 1966 TV and radio personality Chris Evans was born.

2 1947 Country singer Emmylou Harris was born. 1972 Burt Reynolds appeared nude in *Cosmopolitan* magazine.

3 1951 Madcap actor Eddie Murphy was born. 1993 The Grand National was declared void after two false starts.

4 1963 TV presenter Graham Norton was born. 1983 Space Shuttle *Challenger* made its maiden voyage into space.

5 1908 Screen legend Bette Davis was born. 1982 A Royal Navy Task Force set sail to help recapture the Falklands.

6 1896 The first modern Olympic Games were opened in Athens. 1946 Singer David Gilmour was born.

7 1906 Mount Vesuvius erupted. 1939 TV presenter Sir David Frost was born.

8 1892 Screen legend Mary Pickford was born. 1986 Clint Eastwood was elected mayor of Carmel.

9 1865 The American Civil war ended. 1898 Singer Paul Robeson was born.

10 1932 Actor Omar Sharif was born. 1989 Nick Faldo became the first Briton to win golf's US Masters.

11 1929 Popeye made his first public appearance. 1987 Soul sensation Joss Stone was born.

12 1947 Writer Tom Clancy was born. 1961 Yuri Gagarin became the first man in space.

13 1936 Luton's Joe Payne scored a record ten goals in one game. 1946 Singer Al Green was born.

14 1865 Abraham Lincoln was assassinated. 1904 Actor Sir John Gielgud was born.

15 1912 The *Titanic* sank. 1959 Oscar-winning actress Emma Thompson was born.

16 1746 The last battle on British soil was fought – at Culloden. 1918 Funnyman Spike Milligan was born.

17 1956 Premium bonds went on sale for the first time. 1974 Posh Spice, Victoria Beckham was born.

18 1946 Actress Hayley Mills was born. 1994 Cricketer Brian Lara completed a record-breaking Test innings of 375.

19 1935 Funnyman Dudley Moore was born. 1956 Soccer legend Sir Bobby Charlton scored the first of his record 49 goals for England.

20 1941 Actor Ryan O'Neal was born. 1964 BBC2 first went on air.

21 753 BC Romulus founded Rome. 1926 HRH Queen Elizabeth II was born.

22 1936 Singer Glen Campbell was born. 1972 John Fairfax and Sylvia Cook completed their marathon row across the Pacific.

23 1564 Playwright William Shakespeare was born. 1968 Britain's first decimal coins were circulated.

24 1942 Superstar Barbra Streisand was born. 1955 Patrick Moore's *Sky at Night* was first televised.

25 1940 Oscar-winning actor Al Pacino was born. 1982 British troops recaptured South Georgia from Argentina.

26 1938 Guitarist Duane Eddy was born. 1994 The first free elections were held in South Africa.

27 1908 The Olympic Games opened in London. 1922 Actor Jack Klugman was born.

28 1770 Captain Cook landed at Botany Bay. 1937 Oscar-winning actor Jack Nicholson was born.

29 1958 Actress Michelle Pfeiffer was born. 1986 Halley's Comet made its last visit here until the year 2062.

30 1974 *Little Britain*'s Matt Lucas was born. 1975 The Vietnam War ended.

May

1   1931 New York's Empire State Building was opened. 1946 *The Absolutely Fabulous* Joanna Lumley was born.

2   1963 The Beatles had their first UK number one hit. 1985 Singer/songwriter Lily Allen was born.

3   1492 Christopher Columbus arrived in Jamaica instead of China as he'd hoped. 1933 'The Godfather of Soul' James Brown was born.

4   1780 The first Epsom Derby was run. 1929 Screen legend Audrey Hepburn was born.

5   1943 TV globe-trotter Michael Palin was born. 1980 The SAS stormed the Iranian Embassy in London.

6   1895 Screen legend Rudolph Valentino was born. 1994 The Channel Tunnel was officially opened.

7   1756 Nelson's ship HMS *Victory* was launched. 1812 Poet Robert Browning was born.

8   1945 World War II ended. 1975 Singer/songwriter Enrique Iglesias was born.

9   1671 Thomas Blood stole the Crown Jewels from the Tower of London. 1936 Oscar-winning actress and politician Glenda Jackson was born.

10   1857 The Indian Mutiny broke out. 1960 U2's Bono was born.

11   1904 Surrealist painter Salvador Dali was born. 1981 The musical *Cats* opened in London.

12   1937 George VI was crowned. 1968 Funnywoman Catherine Tate was born.

13   1607 Jamestown, the first English settlement in America, was established. 1950 Pop legend Stevie Wonder was born.

14 1796 Physician Edward Jenner used the world's first vaccine. 1969 Oscar-winning actress Cate Blanchett was born.

15 1981 Horseriding royal Zara Phillips was born. 1988 Russia began pulling out of Afghanistan after an eight-year occupation.

16 1905 Screen legend Henry Fonda was born. 1929 The first Oscars were awarded.

17 1911 Actress Maureen O'Sullivan was born. 2000 Alan Chambers and Charlie Paton became the first Britons to walk to the North Pole without backup.

18 1804 Napoleon was proclaimed Emperor of France. 1919 Ballerina Dame Margot Fonteyn was born.

19 1945 The Who's Pete Townsend was born. 1991 Helen Sharman became the first Briton in space.

20 1588 The ill-fated Spanish Armada set sail from Lisbon. 1946 Singer/actress Cher was born.

21 1916 Jazz pianist Fats Waller was born. 1979 Sir Elton John became the first western rock star to perform in Russia.

22 1908 The Wright brothers patented the world's first aeroplane. 1978 TV personality Katie Price (aka Jordan) was born.

23 1498 Vasco da Gama became the first European to reach India by sea. 1936 Actress Joan Collins was born.

24 1844 Samuel Morse sent the world's first telegraph message. 1942 Singer/songwriter Bob Dylan was born.

25 1936 Athlete Jesse Owens set an amazing six world records in 45 minutes. 1958 Singer/songwriter Paul Weller was born.

26 1865 The American Civil War ended. 1948 Singer/songwriter Stevie Nicks was born.

27 1941 The *Bismarck* was sunk. 1975 TV chef Jamie Oliver was born.

28 1967 Sir Francis Chichester completed his round-the-world journey in *Gypsy Moth IV*. 1968 Singer Kylie Minogue was born.

29 1949 Status Quo's Francis Rossi was born. 1953 Sir Edmund Hillary and Sherpa Tenzing conquered Everest.

30 1909 Jazz band leader Benny Goodman was born. 1963 *Coronation Street*'s Sally Webster (alias actress Sally Whittaker) was born.

31 1930 Actor Clint Eastwood was born. 1965 Jim Clark became the first British driver to win the Indianapolis 500.

June

1 1926 Screen legend Marilyn Monroe was born. 1967 The Beatles released their classic album *Sergeant Pepper's Lonely Hearts Club Band.*

2 1941 Rolling Stones' drummer Charlie Watts was born. 1953 HRH Queen Elizabeth II was crowned.

3 1925 Actor Tony Curtis was born. 1981 Shergar won the Derby by a record 10 lengths.

4 1913 Suffragette Emily Davison threw herself under the King's horse in the Derby. 1975 Actress Angelina Jolie was born.

5 1949 Thriller writer Ken Follett was born. 1975 The Suez Canal reopened after eight years' closure.

6 1956 Tennis ace Bjorn Borg was born. 1994 Cricketer Brian Lara completed his record-breaking innings of 501 not out.

7 1848 Post-impressionist painter Paul Gauguin was born.

1982 Elvis Presley's mansion Graceland was opened to the public for the first time.

8 1960 Singer/songwriter Mick Hucknall was born. 1978 Dame Naomi James completed her epic solo circumnavigation of the world.

9 1934 Donald Duck made his film debut. 1963 Actor Johnny Depp was born.

10 1921 HRH Prince Philip, Duke of Edinburgh was born. 1986 Bob Geldof was given an honorary knighthood for his efforts to relieve world famine.

11 1935 Actor Gene Wilder was born. 1975 The first oil was pumped from the North Sea.

12 1929 Diarist Anne Frank was born. 1979 Bryan Allen crossed the Channel in a pedal boat.

13 1865 Poet W.B. Yeats was born. 1900 The Boxer Rising took place in China.

14 1969 Tennis ace Steffi Graf was born. 1982 The Union Jack was hoisted in Port Stanley at the end of the Falklands War.

15 1215 Magna Carta was signed, sealed and delivered. 1954 Actor Jim Belushi was born.

16 1890 Funnyman Stan Laurel was born. 1963 Valentina Tereshkova became the first woman in space.

17 1775 Britain defeated America at the Battle of Bunker Hill. 1882 Composer Igor Stravinsky was born.

18 1815 Napoleon met his Waterloo at Waterloo. 1942 Superstar Sir Paul McCartney was born.

19 1829 Sir Robert Peel founded the Metropolitan Police. 1954 Actress Kathleen Turner was born.

20 1837 Queen Victoria began her 63 year reign. 1966 Actress Nicole Kidman was born.

21 1970 Brazil won soccer's World Cup for the third time and so kept the trophy permanently. 1982 Prince William was born.

22 1937 Joe Louis began his 11-year reign as world heavyweight boxing champion. 1949 Oscar-winning actress Meryl Streep was born.

23 1911 George V was crowned. 1975 Singer/songwriter K T Tunstall was born.

24 1877 The St John Ambulance Brigade was founded. 1944 Rock legend Jeff Beck was born.

25 1876 The Battle of the Little Bighorn was fought. 1903 Writer George Orwell was born.

26 1857 The first Victoria Cross was awarded. 1956 Singer Chris Isaak was born.

27 1962 Singer Michael Ball was born. 1988 Dave Hurst and Alan Matthews became the first blind mountaineers to scale Mont Blanc.

28 1491 Henry VIII was born. 1997 The British Lions roared to their first series win over South Africa for 25 years.

29 1577 Painter Sir Peter Paul Rubens was born. 1613 Shakespeare's Globe Theatre was burnt down.

30 1966 Boxer Mike Tyson was born. 1997 Britain handed Hong Kong back to China.

July

1 1838 Charles Darwin first expounded his theory of evolution. 1961 Princess Diana was born.

2 1865 William Booth founded the Salvation Army. 1973 Funnyman Peter Kay was born.

3 1898 Joshua Slocum became the first solo round-the-world yachtsman. 1962 Actor Tom Cruise was born.

4 1776 The American Declaration of Independence was approved by Congress. 1962 Actor Neil Morrissey was born (behaving badly, of course).

5 1969 Over a quarter of a million fans crowded into Hyde Park for a free Rolling Stones concert. 1979 Westlife's Shane Filan was born.

6 1685 The Battle of Sedgemoor – the last battle on English soil – was fought. 1946 John J. Rambo (alias actor Sylvester Stallone) was born.

7 1940 Drummer Ringo Starr was born. 1988 Live Aid concerts in London and Philadelphia raised millions for famine relief.

8 1951 Actress Anjelica Huston was born. 1978 Reinhold Messner and Peter Habeler became the first mountaineers to climb Everest without the use of oxygen.

9 1947 The betrothal of the future Queen Elizabeth II to Lieutenant Philip Mountbatten was announced. 1956 Actor Tom Hanks was born.

10 1900 The Paris Metro was opened. 1962 TV personality Gaby Roslin was born.

11 1950 Andy Pandy made his TV debut. 1959 Singer Suzanne Vega was born.

12 1958 The *Absolutely Fabulous* Jennifer Saunders was born. 1982 The Falklands War officially ended.

13 1942 Actor Harrison Ford was born. 1985 Live Aid pop concerts raised millions for African famine victims.

14 1789 The Bastille was stormed. 1950 Fashion designer Bruce Oldfield was born.

15 1881 Sheriff Pat Garrett shot Billy the Kid. 1946 Singer Linda Ronstadt was born.

16 1790 Washington DC became the capital of the USA. 1907 Screen legend Barbara Stanwyck was born.

17 1917 The British Royal Family changed its name to Windsor. 1952 Actor David Hasselhoff was born.

18 1941 Singer Martha Reeves was born. 1955 Disneyland was opened in California.

19 1545 Henry VIII's battleship the *Mary Rose* sank in the Solent. 1969 Singer Gabrielle was born.

20 1837 London's Euston Station was opened. 1946 Former *Eastender* Pauline Fowler (alias actress Wendy Richard) was born.

21 1952 Funnyman Robin Williams was born. 1969 Astronaut Neil Armstrong took a giant leap for mankind.

22 The Reverend William Spooner, originator of spoonerisms, was porn in Breston. 1934 'Public Enemy No. 1' John Dillinger was shot dead by the FBI.

23 1759 Construction of Nelson's flagship, HMS *Victory* began. 1947 Singer/actor David Essex was born.

24 1936 The Speaking Clock spoke for the first time. 1970 Singer Jennifer Lopez was born.

25 1909 Louis Bleriot made the first cross-Channel flight. 1978 Britain's first test tube baby, Louise Joy Brown, was born.

26 1908 The FBI was founded in Washington. 1965 Hollywood actress Sandra Bullock was born.

27 1937 Actor Bill Cosby was born. 1953 The Korean War ended.

28 1936 Cricket legend Sir Garfield Sobers was born. 1996 Rower Steve Redgrave clinched his fourth successive Olympic gold medal at Atlanta.

29 1558 Sir Francis Drake completed his game of bowls before going on to defeat the Spanish Armada. 1905 Silent film star Clara Bow was born.

30 1947 Iron-pumping Arnold Schwarzenegger was born. 1966 England won soccer's World Cup.

31 1956 Jim Laker completed his record-breaking 19 for 90 haul against the Aussies. 1967 TV Superman Dean Cain was born.

August

1 1798 Nelson won the Battle of the Nile. 1963 Chart rapper Coolio was born.

2 1876 Wild Bill Hickok was shot by Jack McCall in Deadwood. 1932 Actor Peter O'Toole was born.

3 1778 La Scala Opera House opened in Milan. 1940 Actor Martin Sheen was born.

4 1914 World War I began. 1943 Actress Georgina Hale was born.

5 1901 Britain's first cinema opened. 1906 Supersleuth Miss Jane Marple (alias actress Joan Hickson) was born.

6 1926 Gertrude Ederle became the first woman to swim the Channel. 1937 *Eastenders*' Peggy Mitchell (alias actress Barbara Windsor) was born.

7 1840 The employment of boys as chimney sweeps was banned. 1960 *X Files* star David Duchovny was born.

8 1961 U2 guitarist The Edge was born. 1963 The Great Train Robbery took place.

9 1968 *X Files* star Gillian Anderson was born. 1979 Nude sun bathing became legal on Cliff Beach, Brighton.

10 1675 The Royal Observatory at Greenwich was opened. 1947 Jethro Tull's Ian Anderson was born.

11 1942 London's New Waterloo Bridge was opened. 1954 Singer Joe Jackson was born.

12 1908 The first Model T Ford car was produced. 1949 Dire Straits' Mark Knopfler was born.

13 1704 The Duke of Marlborough won the Battle of Blenheim. 1958 Singer Feargal Sharkey was born.

14 1945 Japan surrendered unconditionally thereby ending World War II. 1968 Oscar-winning actress Halle Berry was born.

15 1969 The first Woodstock rock festival opened in upstate New York. 1972 Boyzone's Mikey Graham was born.

16 1958 Madonna (the outrageous singer, not the outrageous footballer) was born. 1975 Phil Collins became Genesis's lead singer.

17 1896 The Canadian Klondike Goldrush began. 1943 Actor Robert De Niro was born.

18 1937 Actor Robert Redford was born. 1948 12-year-old Lester Piggott rode his first winner.

19 1897 Electric cabs began running in London. 1969 *Friends*' star Matthew Perry was born.

20 1924 Eric Liddell refused to enter the Olympic 100-metres heats as it was a Sunday. 1971 *Little Britain*'s David Walliams was born.

21 1933 Film buff Barry Norman was born – and why not? 1988 Pubs were first allowed to stay open 12 hours a day.

22 1642 The English Civil War began. 1961 Tears For Fears' Roland Orzabel was born.

23 1938 Len Hutton scored a record 364 runs against the Aussies. 1962 Singer Shaun Ryder was born.

24 79 AD Pompeii was destroyed by the eruption of Vesuvius. 1958 Actor Steve Guttenberg was born.

25 1875 Captain Matthew Webb was the first person to swim the English Channel. 1953 Singer/songwriter Elvis Costello was born.

26 55 BC Julius Caesar came, saw and conquered. 1954 DJ Steve Wright was born – in the afternoon of course.

27 1883 Krakatoa erupted. 1908 Cricket legend Sir Don Bradman was born.

28 1961 Singer Kim Appleby was born. 1963 Dr Martin Luther King delivered his famous 'I have a dream' speech in Washington.

29 1915 Swedish actress Ingrid Bergman was born. 1966 The Beatles played their final live concert – at Candlestick Park, San Francisco.

30 1860 Britain's first tramcar took to the streets – in Birkenhead. 1955 Swing Out Sister's Martin Jackson was born.

31 1949 Actor Richard Gere was born. 1968 Cricketer Gary Sobers smashed six sixes in an over for Nottinghamshire.

September

1 1957 Singer Gloria Estefan was born. 1972 Bobby Fisher became world chess champion.

2 1952 Tennis ace Jimmy Connors was born. 1995 Frank Bruno became world heavyweight boxing champion.

3 1939 Britain declared war on Hitler's Germany. 1965 Actor Charlie Sheen was born.

4 1949 American golfer Tom Watson was born. 1964 The Forth Road Bridge was opened.

5 1885 Arbroath hammered Bon Accord by a record 36–0. 1940 Actress Raquel Welch was born.

6 1620 The *Mayflower* set sail for the New World. 1944 Singer Roger Waters was born.

7 1951 Rocker Chrissie Hynde was born. 1986 Bishop Desmond Tutu was enthroned as Archbishop of Cape Town.

8 1664 New Amsterdam was captured by Britain and

renamed New York. 1946 Rock legend Freddie Mercury was born.

9   1960 Actor Hugh Grant was born. 1978 Eighteen-year-old Czech tennis star Martina Navratilova asked for political asylum in America.

10   1953 Hollywood star Amy Irving was born. 1967 Gibraltar voted overwhelmingly to remain British.

11   1940 Film director Brian De Palma was born. 1978 The BBC broadcast the first episode of *Dallas*.

12   2005 England won the Ashes for the first time since 1987. 1957 Actress Rachel Ward was born.

13   1957 *The Mousetrap* became Britain's longest-running West End play. 1959 Impressionist Bobby Davro was born.

14   1752 Britain adopted the Gregorian calendar. 1983 Singer/songwriter Amy Winehouse was born.

15   1940 Britain won the Battle of Britain. 1946 Film director Oliver Stone was born.

16   1927 Lieutenant Columbo (alias actor Peter Falk) was born. 1968 The Post Office introduced its two-tier delivery service.

17   1931 Long-playing records were invented. 1969 The Prodigy singer Keith Flint was born.

18   1879 The Blackpool illuminations were first switched on. 1967 Actress Tara Fitzgerald was born.

19   1963 Pulp singer Jarvis Cocker was born. 1975 The first episode of *Fawlty Towers* was televised.

20   1934 Actress Sophia Loren was born. 1967 The *QEII* was launched.

21   1965 BP struck oil in the North Sea. 1972 Oasis singer Liam Gallagher was born.

22 1955 Commercial television began in Britain. 1971 Singer Chesney Hawkes was born.

23 1949 The Boss, Bruce Springsteen, was born in the USA. 1964 Zero Mostel sang 'If I were a rich man' in the first performance of *Fiddler on the Roof.*

24 1962 Funnyman Jack Dee was born. 1975 Dougal Haston and Doug Scott made the first all-British ascent of Everest.

25 1066 The Battle of Stamford Bridge took place (no, Chelsea weren't playing). 1969 *Men in Black* star Will Smith was born.

26 1934 The *Queen Mary* was launched. 1945 Singer Bryan Ferry was born.

27 1825 The Stockton to Darlington rail line was opened. 1947 Rocker Meat Loaf was born.

28 1972 Oscar-winning actress Gwyneth Paltrow was born. 1996 Jockey Frankie Dettori rode all seven winners at Ascot.

29 1970 Actress Emily Lloyd was born. 1983 Lady Mary Donaldson was elected first woman Lord Mayor of London.

30 1967 Radio 1 first went on air. 1980 Tennis ace Martina Hingis was born.

October

1 1964 Wacky comic Harry Hill was born. 1971 Disney World opened in Florida.

2 1950 Charlie Brown and Snoopy made their first public appearance. 1951 Singer Sting was born.

3 1899 The Boer War began. 1941 Pop twister Chubby Checker was born.

4 1957 *Sputnik*, the first satellite to orbit earth, was launched. 1976 Batgirl Alicia Silverstone was born.

5 1936 The Jarrow March began. 1954 Rocker Sir Bob Geldof was born.

6 1930 *Coronation Street*'s, Emily Bishop (alias actress Eileen Derbyshire) was born. 1985 Nigel Mansell won his first Grand Prix.

7 1769 Captain Cook landed in New Zealand. 1959 *The X Factor*'s Mr Nasty, Simon Cowell, was born.

8 1949 *Aliens* star Sigourney Weaver was born. 1965 London's Post Office Tower was opened.

9 1888 The Washington Monument was unveiled. 1940 Pop legend John Lennon was born.

10 1946 Actor Charles Dance was born. 1972 Sir John Betjeman was appointed Poet Laureate.

11 1957 Comedienne Dawn French was born. 1982 Henry VIII's war ship *Mary Rose* was raised from Portsmouth Harbour.

12 1954 Entertainer Les Dennis was born. 1986 Queen Elizabeth II became the first British monarch to visit China.

13 1941 Singer/songwriter Paul Simon was born. 1997 Andy Green broke the sound barrier in his supersonic car Thrust.

14 1066 The Battle of Hastings was fought. 1940 Peter Pan pop singer Sir Cliff Richard was born.

15 1948 Singer Chris de Burgh was born. 1962 Amnesty International was founded in London.

16 1815 Napoleon was exiled to St Helena. 1925 Cabot Cove's Jessica Fletcher (alias actress Angela Lansbury) was born.

17 1931 Al Capone was sentenced to 11 years' imprisonment for income tax evasion. 1972 Rap artist Eminem was born.

18 1887 The USA bought Alaska from Russia for 7 million dollars. 1960 Actor Jean-Claude Van Damme was born.

19 1812 Napoleon began his retreat from Moscow. 1963 Singer Sinitta was born.

20 1946 Muffin the Mule made his TV debut. 1958 Level 42's Mark King was born.

21 1805 Nelson was killed at Trafalgar. 1957 Pop star Julian Cope was born.

22 1797 André-Jacques Garnerin made the first-ever parachute jump. 1968 Chart-topper Shaggy was born.

23 1642 The Battle of Edgehill was fought. 1940 Soccer legend Pelé was born.

24 1945 The United Nations came into existence. 1985 Soccer's Wayne Rooney was born.

25 1415 Henry V defeated the French at Agincourt. 1962 TV host Nick Hancock was born.

26 1881 The Gunfight at the OK Corral took place. 1957 Actress Julie Dawn Cole was born.

27 1958 *Blue Peter* was first televised. 1978 Violinist Vanessa-Mae was born.

28 1949 Sooty and Sweep made their television debut. 1967 *Pretty Woman* star Julia Roberts was born.

29 1929 Panic selling on the New York Stock Exchange led to the Wall Street Crash. 1947 Actor Richard Dreyfuss was born.

30 1938 People thought Martians had landed when Orson Welles read *The War of the Worlds* on US radio. 1943 Singer Grace Slick was born.

31 1951 Zebra crossings were introduced in Britain. 1961 U2's Larry Mullen was born.

November

1   1512 Michelangelo unveiled the ceiling of the Sistine Chapel. 1963 Def Leppard's Rick Allen was born.

2   1961 Singer k. d. lang was born. 1964 The first episode of *Crossroads* was broadcast.

3   1921 *Death Wish* star Charles Bronson was born. 1957 Laika became the first dog in space.

4   1605 Guy Fawkes was arrested for attempting to blow up Parliament – yes, it was on the *4th* November. 1979 Chart star Kavana was born.

5   1909 Britain's first Woolworth store was opened – in Liverpool. 1959 Singer Bryan Adams was born.

6   1951 Actor Niger Havers was born. 1988 US Defence department computers were crippled by a virus introduced by an employee's son.

7   1917 The October Revolution (yes October) began in Russia. 1943 Singer/songwriter Joni Mitchell was born.

8   1946 Rocker Roy Wood was born. 1974 Lord Lucan disappeared.

9   1951 *Incredible Hulk* star Lou Ferrigno was born. 1960 John F. Kennedy was elected US President.

10   1944 Songwriter Sir Tim Rice was born. 1989 The hated Berlin Wall was dismantled.

11   1918 World War I ended. 1974 *Titanic* star Leonardo DiCaprio was born.

12   1927 The first veteran car rally from London to Brighton took place. 1945 Singer Neil Young was born.

13   1914 Mrs Mary Phelps Jacob patented her new uplifting invention – the bra. 1949 Actress Whoopi Goldberg was born.

14   1953 Singer Alexander O'Neal was born. 1994 The first public train service ran – or rather crawled – through the Channel Tunnel.

15 1945 ABBA's Anna-Frid Lingstad was born. 1969 Britain's first colour TV advertisement was screened, mainly in green – it was for Birds Eye Peas.

16 1532 Spanish adventurer Pizarro conquered the Incas. 1961 Boxer Frank Bruno was born (Know what I mean, 'Arry?).

17 1869 The Suez Canal was opened. 1960 TV and radio presenter Jonathan Ross was born.

18 1928 Mickey Mouse made his film debut. 1960 Singer Kim Wilde was born.

19 1961 Actress Meg Ryan was born. 1994 The first National Lottery draw was made.

20 1947 Princess Elizabeth married Lieutenant Philip Mountbatten.1956 Actress Bo Derek was born.

21 1620 *The Mayflower* arrived in the New World. 1965 Singer Bjork was born.

22 1958 Actress Jamie Lee Curtis was born. 2003 England won the Rugby World Cup.

23 1943 *Coronation Street*'s Audrey Roberts (alias actress Sue Nicholls) was born. 1963 *Dr Who*'s Tardis materialised for the first time.

24 1942 Funnyman Billy Connolly was born. 1952 Agatha Christie's play *The Mousetrap* opened at the Ambassadors Theatre, London.

25 1944 ELO's drummer Bev Bevan was born. 1953 England put three goals past Hungary at Wembley – but let in six.

26 1938 Simply the Best singer Tina Turner was born. 1968 Supergroup Cream played their final concert at London's Albert Hall.

27 1582 Shakespeare married Anne Hathaway. 1942 Pop legend Jimi Hendrix was born.

28 1961 Actor/comedian Martin Clunes was born. 1990 Maggie Thatcher resigned as Prime Minister.

29 1962 Britain and France agreed to build Concorde. 1973 Soccer's Ryan Giggs dribbled for the first time.

30 1936 The Crystal Palace was burnt down in a spectacular fire. 1945 Deep Purple's Roger Glover was born.

December

1 1887 The first Sherlock Holmes story was published. 1940 Comic Richard Pryor was born.

2 1697 Sir Christopher Wren's new St Paul's Cathedral was opened. 1960 Def Leppard's Rick Savage was born.

3 1948 Rocker Ozzie Osbourne was born. 1967 Dr Christian Barnard performed the world's first heart transplant operation.

4 1937 The first edition of the *Dandy* was published. 1949 Actor Jeff Bridges was born.

5 1872 The *Marie Celeste* was found adrift and unmanned near the Azores. 1935 Rock legend Little Richard was born.

6 1877 Thomas Edison made the first sound recording. 1920 Jazzman Dave Brubeck was born.

7 1941 Japan attacked the US fleet at Pearl Harbor. 1949 Singer Tom Waits was born.

8 1863 Britain's Tom King (the boxer, not the politician) became the first world heavyweight champion. 1953 Actress Kim Basinger was born.

9 1950 Singer Joan Armatrading was born. 1960 The first episode of *Coronation Street* was broadcast.

10 1901 Nobel Prizes were first awarded. 1952 TV personality Clive Anderson was born.

11 1936 King Edward VIII gave up the crown so he could marry Wallis Simpson. 1942 Actress Anna Carteret was born.

12 1901 Marconi made the first transatlantic wireless

transmission. 1915 The late and great Frank Sinatra was born.

13   1577 Sir Francis Drake began his circumnavigation of the world in the *Golden Hind*. 1953 Entertainer Jim Davidson was born.

14   1911 Roald Amundsen became the first man to reach the South Pole. 1979 Soccer's Michael Owen dribbled for the first time.

15   1964 *Coronation Street*'s Kevin Webster (alias actor Michael Le Veil) was born. 1979 Two Canadian journalists thought up the game of Trivial Pursuit.

16   1773 The Boston Tea Party took place. 1949 ZZ Top's Billy Gibbons was born.

17   1903 Orville Wright made the first ever aeroplane flight. 1969 Supergrass rocker Mickey Quinn was born.

18   1865 Slavery was abolished in the USA. 1947 Film director Steven Spielberg was born.

19   1963 *Flashdance* star Jennifer Beals was born. 1984 Britain agreed to return Hong Kong to China.

20   1803 The biggest land deal in history – The Louisiana Purchase – doubled the size of the USA at the stroke of a quill. 1946 Fork-bending Uri Geller was born.

21   1913 The world's first crossword puzzle was published. 1940 Rock legend Frank Zappa was born.

22   1895 Wilhelm Rtintgen discovered X-rays. 1946 *Deal or No Deal*'s Noel Edmonds was born.

23   1888 Vincent Van Gogh cut off part of his left ear. 1955 Iron Maiden's Dave Murray was born.

24   1945 Motorhead's Lemmy was born. 1968 *Apollo 8* became the first manned spaceship to orbit the moon.

25 1066 William the Conquerer was crowned at Westminster Abbey. 1949 Actress Sissy Spacek was born.

26 1906 The world's first feature length film was shown in Australia. 1927 Actor Denis Quilley was born.

27 1904 J. M. Barrie's *Peter Pan* had its first night. 1948 French actor Gerard Depardieu was born.

28 1879 The Tay Bridge collapsed, leading to that terrible poem by William McGonagall. 1981 Actress Sienna Miller was born.

29 1930 Radio Luxembourg first went on air. 1972 Actor Jude Law was born.

30 1916 Russian mystic Rasputin was poisoned, shot and, for good measure, drowned. 1928 Rock legend Bo Diddley was born.

31 1923 The chimes of Big Ben were heard by radio listeners for the first time. 1958 Actor Val Kilmer was born.

HOOKING WITH BRACKETS

Bracketing is a device usually associated with seasoned pros. It requires far more thought and planning than the other hooks because it is designed not only to grab an audience's attention at the *start* of a speech, but also – and at the same time – to set up a situation that can be exploited at the *end*. The idea is to present your speech as a satisfying whole, not just as a series of jokes, quotes and sentimental reminiscences.

The two brackets consist of a **set-up** at the opening of the speech and a **payoff** at the end. The words you will end with include those planted clearly at the start, like this:

Set-up: Ladies and Gentlemen, when this little do ends, Gary and Dorothy are off to Iceland. What better place to enjoy an Eskimo roll? He almost went to Iceland once before, but they were closed so he went to Tesco instead.

That's your first bracket. You've set up the situation briefly and then quickly reinforced it with two one-liners to make it more memorable. It's a pretty good humour hook in its own right, but there's more to come.

Pay-off: Well now that Iceland honeymoon and Eskimo roll await them, so I suppose Gary will be kissed in places he's only ever dreamt of before. [*followed by the toast*]

Notice the repetition of the planted words *Iceland* and *Eskimo roll*. This helps the open-and-closed nature of the brackets and provides a pleasing symmetry.

This technique can also be used to begin a quotation in your opening, and then complete it at the end. Here's an example:

Set-up: I am yours, you are mine. Of this we are certain. You are lodged in my heart. Ladies and Gentlemen . . .

Pay-off: I am yours, you are mine. Of this we are certain. You are lodged in my heart, the small key is lost. You must stay forever.

Or you could use it to add a little compliment to sugar the teasing joke you opened with. How about this sort of thing for the sporty types?

Set-up: Ladies and Gentlemen, as Boris left the church today I heard him ask the vicar if he'd be committing a sin if he played tennis on the Sabbath. The vicar replied, 'The way you play, it would be a sin on any day.' But Boris is improving. He practises by hitting a tennis ball against his garage door. It's really improved his game. He hasn't won yet, but last week he took the door to five sets.

Payoff: Boris and Steffi are excellent tennis players who are both game and set for the perfect match.

You can get ideas for humorous, romantic or sentimental brackets simply by listening to songs composed by the best popular lyricists of yesterday and today: Noel Coward, Ira Gershwin, Cole Porter, Jim Webb, Bob Dylan, Lou Read, Morrisey – to name but a few. This is how master songsmith Sammy Cahn achieved a neat little twist in the tail of *Call Me Irresponsible*:

Set-up: Call me irresponsible, call me unreliable, throw in undependable too.

Payoff: Call me irresponsible, yes I'm unreliable, but it's undeniably true: I'm irresponsibly mad for you.

If you make use of a lyricist's brackets, always reword them into the kind of language you use, making sure that they no longer rhyme. In this way your audience won't recognise your source – or your sauce – and you are sure to come across as a natural and original speaker.

It is quite easy to adapt and paraphrase musical brackets to suit your speech. Let's take a more up-to-date example. These are the set-up and payoff lines used by Rupert Holmes in *Nearsighted*.

Set-up: If you take these glasses from my face I think that you will find I'm undeniably, certifiably just a shade of blind. The day is brighter, somewhat lighter, when it's slightly blurred. Nearsighted, it's another lovely day, so I stumble on my way.

Payoff: Nearsighted: loving life is such a breeze. Nearsighted: I see just what I please – and it pleases me to see you. Though I'm slightly out of focus, I can see my dreams come true. Nearsighted, all I need to see is you.

This is how a bespectacled groom might adapt, develop and paraphrase these brackets:

Set-up: Ladies and Gentlemen, if I take off my glasses I can't see very far ahead. In the past I've often been shortsighted and stumbled my way through life. But today I can see the way ahead clearly.

Payoff: You know, I don't need these glasses to see a bright future for us. Shortsighted? [*remove your glasses*] Who cares? All I need to see is you.

Bracketing is a wonderful way of linking attention-grabbing openings with emotion-packed big finishes.

ENDING ON THE RIGHT NOTE

A wedding speech is like a love affair. Any fool can start it, but to end it requires considerable skill. Film producer Sam Goldwyn once told a scriptwriter: 'What we want is a story that starts with an earthquake and works its way up to a climax.' It's the same with your speech. Begin with a great hook, then say a few sincere and entertaining words which strike the right balance of seriousness and humour, and then deliver a final round verbal KO.

As well as the bracketing hook close which, by definition, should already include a big finish, the humour hook, quotation hook and anniversary hook can all easily be adapted to serve as powerful closes. Here is an example of each:

> I leave you with this thought. There are Seven Deadly Sins, enough for one each day – or night. Have a nice week's honeymoon!

> It has been said that there is only one happiness in life: to love and be loved. Today Carol and Alan found their happiness.

> This day, the 18th of December, will always be remembered because of three famous events. Slavery was abolished in America in 1865, film director Steven Spielberg was born in 1947, and on this very day in 200X, Ross married Emily!

There are four other classic closes that would help make any wedding speech memorable:

- ◆ the sentimental close

- ◆ the inspirational close

- ◆ the shock close

- ◆ the wit and wisdom close.

Let's take a look at each in turn.

The sentimental close

This is a close that can work wonderfully for the bride's father or for the bridegroom, but *not* for the best man who should steer well clear of anything remotely emotional or serious in his speech. If you mean it deeply, then say it from the heart:

Jayne, I love you.

The inspirational close

This is another device that the best man should avoid. We can learn much from the great inspirational speakers of past and present: Sir Winston Churchill, John F. Kennedy, Mahatma Gandhi, Nelson Mandela. If you find an ideal uplifting line that would wrap up your speech perfectly, then grab it, adapt it and use it.

Martin Luther King concluded his famous 'I have a dream' speech with these words:

Free at last! Free at last! Thank God Almighty, Free at last!

This powerful three-phrase close could be adapted to:

Together at last! Together at last! Thank God, we are together at last!

The shock close

The idea here is to make an apparently outrageous or shocking statement. Then, after a brief pause, to clarify yourself. Your audience's relief will be audible.

Finally, I have a confession to make. When I took my vows in church today, I lied. I did *not* marry for better or for worse – I married for good!

The wit and wisdom close

Some speakers end with a good joke while others prefer to impart a pearl of wisdom. Why not do both? Why not use humour to illustrate a universal truth? These three gems come from Bob Monkhouse, Groucho Marx and Pam Ayres:

Marriage is an investment that pays dividends if you pay interest.

Woman lies to man. Man lies to woman. But the best part is when they lie together.

Love is like a curry and I'll explain to you, That love comes in three temperatures: medium, hot and vindaloo.

Whichever close you chose, make sure you end on a note of high emotion or with a witty, wise or uplifting little quote or story that will leave them gobsmacked. And finally, where appropriate, don't forget to propose that toast!

2

Turning Listeners into Participants

The starter and dessert are now well prepared and it is time to turn attention to the main course. Recipe for a great little speech? No waffle and plenty of shortening. The ingredients required are humour and seriousness, all applied with liberal helpings of sentiment.

Your aim is to communicate with your audience – to establish a dialogue with them – to turn listeners into participants. How? By involving them. By making them laugh. By making them cry. By allowing them not only to hear your speech but also to *experience* it.

As you plan and prepare the middle section of your speech, remember these three little words:

KISS THE BRIDE

This will remind you of two vital things. Firstly, the word KISS will remind you to:

Keep
It
Short and
Simple

Don't suffer from the illusion that you can make your speech immortal by making it everlasting. In the Bible, the story of the Creation is told in 400 words (that's about 3 minutes) and the Ten Commandments are covered in less than 300. Try to say everything you need to in less than 650 words (5 minutes). Size *does* matter. And no speech can be entirely bad if it's short enough.

Secondly, **THE BRIDE** will remind you that it is *her* big day. Don't spoil it by embarrassing her or by knocking the institution of marriage.

KISS THE BRIDE and you can't go far wrong!

KNOWING YOUR PURPOSE AND MESSAGE

The main purpose of a wedding speech is to propose a toast or to respond to one, or to do both. The usual sequence is:

♦ *Speech 1:* Proposal of a toast to the bride and groom.

♦ *Speech 2:* Response to the toast and then proposal of a second toast.

♦ *Speech 3:* Response to the second toast on behalf of the bridesmaids.

Traditionally, the bride's father (or a close relative or family friend) makes the first speech; the bridegroom makes the second (making it clear that he is also speaking on behalf of his wife); and the best man makes the third. However, it is perfectly acceptable for other people to speak instead of or as well as these. It all depends on the particular circumstances and backgrounds of the newlyweds. We will consider this in more detail in Chapter 8. At this stage all you need to bear in mind is that if you speak you must know your precise purpose. And it will be to propose a toast, to respond to a toast, or to do both.

While every wedding speech should include a few sincere, optimistic and entertaining words, there are some subtle differences in the messages expected from the three main speakers, as follows:

Bride's father

This speech should contain some positive thoughts about the couple and about love and marriage in general. It should strike a nice balance of humour, emotion and seriousness. He could:

♦ Thank everyone for coming to celebrate his daughter's happy day.

♦ Say a few affectionate words about the bride and bridegroom.

♦ Talk of the happiness he and his wife have experienced in bringing up their daughter. What a treasure she has been to them!

♦ Relate one or two amusing or serious incidents from her childhood.

♦ Stress his positive feelings about his new son-in-law ('I am not losing a daughter; I am gaining a son').

- Offer some (possibly amusing) thoughts about love and what makes a happy marriage.

- Declare his confidence that the bride and groom will make all the effort needed and will not be found wanting.

Bridegroom

This is really a general thank you speech which should also combine elements of humour, emotion and seriousness. He could:

- Say he is also speaking on behalf of his wife ('My wife and I . . .).

- Thank the bride's father for his kind remarks and good wishes, and also for laying on this reception.

- Thank both mothers for their help (whether they have or not).

- Thank the bride's parents for letting him marry their daughter, referring to anything they may have provided for the couple's future.

- Add a few affectionate words about his own parents, perhaps including 'thank you for having me' or a reference to their kindness, care and attention during his boyhood.

- Acknowledge the invaluable services of the best man, and possibly also the chief bridesmaid.

- Thank the guests for their presence – and for their generous gifts.

♦ Tell everyone how lucky he is to marry such a wonderful bride, possibly relating a short, amusing episode involving their first meeting or engagement. He will dedicate himself to her happiness.

♦ Conclude with some complimentary words about the bridesmaids (calling them *charming* and *delightful* is safer than calling them *beautiful*).

Best man

This is a response on behalf of all the attendants. Unlike the first two speakers, he should not say anything too serious or emotional. He could:

♦ Thank the bridegroom for the toast to the bridesmaids.

♦ Add a few complimentary comments of his own about them.

♦ Make a few light-hearted remarks about the bridegroom (positive remarks with absolutely no references to any past flames).

♦ Offer some sincere and complimentary thoughts about the groom and the bride.

♦ Congratulate the bridegroom on his good luck and wish the couple happiness for the future.

♦ Read the tele-messages (having first checked that they are suitable for public consumption), possibly making up the final one, claiming it is from some famous and long-dead person. ('And finally, here's one from Henry VIII. It says, "Congratulations, this is the happiest day of your lives – and good luck for your wedding tomorrow!"').

SELECTING MATERIAL

So what sorts of things should you say? I'm not ducking the question by answering that, this must be up to you. Every speech is different, every audience is different and every speaker is different. However, there are certain common themes that can be identified in all successful wedding speeches. As we have seen, the bride's father and the groom must always give them a mixture of material that will at one moment tug at the heartstrings and at the next have them laughing in the aisles; the best man must always stick to light-hearted and upbeat material. The other common themes that emerge are that they all contain sincere, optimistic and entertaining words and they are *never* boring.

You may already have a pretty good idea of the areas you are going to cover. If so, fine. If not, the best way to recall some humorous or serious episodes involving the bride or groom is to think about one or two of these memory joggers.

Memory joggers

Birthdays	Holidays
Turning Points	Christmas
Major decisions	Friends
School	Hobbies
College	Ambitions
First job	Games and toys
Illness	Pets
Influential people	Travel

Pour yourself a drink, take a hot bath or go for a long walk and the memories will come flooding back. Make a note of them before they're forgotten once again.

Better still, sleep on it. You really will get some of your best ideas this way. Your subconscious mind will take over and will come up with a whole series of interesting and unexpected memories and connections. That's how Robert Louis Stevenson came up with his plots for *Treasure Island* and *Dr Jekyll and Mr Hyde*.

Once you have recalled a few amusing, poignant and illuminating recollections you will need to think about the best way of putting them across to ensure they have the most humorous or emotional impact on your audience. At this stage work on each anecdote, joke and reminiscence in isolation. We'll see how you can thread them all together towards the end of this chapter.

USING WORDS TO BE SAID, NOT READ

Most people can write something to be *read*; few can write something to be *said*. Indeed, most people are unaware that there is even a difference.

We are used to writing things to be read: by our teachers, our friends, our relatives, our bosses, our subordinates. Such everyday written communication is known as **text**. What we are not used to doing is speaking our written words out loud. Writing intended to be spoken and heard is known as **script**.

Every effective speechmaker *must* recognise that there are very important differences between text and script, namely:

Text	**Script**
◆ is a journey at the reader's pace	◆ is a journey at the presenter's pace
◆ can be re-read, if necessary	◆ is heard once, and once only
◆ can be read in any order.	◆ is heard in the order it is presented.

Therefore you must prepare and present a speech for an audience which *cannot* listen at its own pace; which *cannot* ask you to repeat parts it did not hear or understand; and which *cannot* choose the order in which to consider your words.

We seem subconsciously to understand the best words and phrases and the best order of words and phrases when we speak, but we seem to lose the knack when we write script. Consider how the same sentiment might be conveyed by a writer, first using text and then script:

Text:

The meaning of marriage is not to be found in church services, or in romantic novels or films. We have no right to expect a happy ending. The meaning of marriage is to be found in all the effort that is required to make a marriage succeed. You need to get to know your partner, and thereby to get to know yourself.

Script:

The meaning of marriage isn't to be found in wedding bells ... it isn't the stuff of Mills and Boon romances ... there is no happy ever after. No, the meaning of marriage is in the *trying* and it's about learning about someone else . . . and through that learning about yourself.

The lesson is clear: Speak your words out loud before you commit them to paper. You will find that each element, each phrase, each sentence, will be built from what has gone before. Instinctively, you will take your listeners from the *known* to the *unknown*; from the *general* to the *particular*; from the *present* to the *future*.

As a speechwriter you must:

♦ think like the listener, and

♦ write like a talker.

Varying pace
You will need to slow down a little from your normal speaking speed to give your audience time to think about what you are saying. Vary this speed to maintain interest and highlight your most important messages. We will come back to this in Chapter 5.

No replays
Your audience gets just one chance to take in what you are saying. Keep it short and simple, or, as Americans put it: lean and mean. Use an everyday, chatty conversational English because that is the language of easy communication. And easy communication is what speech-making is all about. Advertisers know this, and we can learn a lot from them. This is the script for a TV and radio advert:

Orange believe you shouldn't be rushed into anything.
Which is why we offer a 14-day money-back guarantee.
The future's bright. The future's Orange.

This is English written to be read out loud. It includes:

♦ one simple idea

♦ short words

♦ short sentences (average 8 words)

♦ a link (*Which is why . . .*)

♦ effective repetition (*The future's* bright. *The future's*
Orange)

♦ a reference to the audience (Orange believe *you . . .*).

It is an example of the kind of style you should adopt when
writing your script.

Arranging the order
Arrange your speech in a logical order and always speak your
most important words *first*. If you say:

Jimmy, Ken, Mark, Steve and Ronnie have all beaten Bill
at snooker.

Your audience won't know why you have named all these
people until the very last word of your sentence – and by
then they will have probably forgotten who you mentioned
anyway. For this reason it would be far better to say:

Bill has been beaten at snooker by Jimmy, Ken, Mark, Steve and Ronnie.

Text, script and cue card

The rule is: write your text, transform it to script, reduce it to a cue card with a few memory-jogging keywords and phrases (see Figure 1).

It is important to get your opening and closing lines spot on. For that reason you should *memorise* them. However, it is far better to simply *familiarise* yourself with the middle section of your speech. In this way you are sure to come across as a far more natural and spontaneous speaker because you will be using your own words and phrases, not reciting a prepared speech. That's why cue cards are so useful.

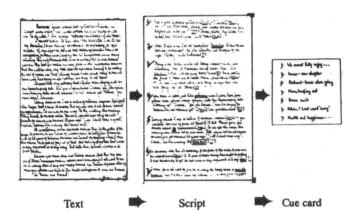

Text ➡ Script ➡ Cue card

Fig. 1. Text, script and cue card.

What you must avoid is talking a lot without saying very much. Your aim is to say a great deal with just a few words. Listen to great raconteurs to see how they do it. Sir Peter Ustinov brought his anecdotes and reminiscences to life, giving them a lyrical, almost magical quality. You can do the same by:

♦ painting word pictures

♦ using figurative language

♦ engaging all the senses

♦ using symbolism

♦ remembering rhythm.

PAINTING WORD PICTURES

People today spend more time *watching* TV or films than *listening* to the radio. They are used to visual images so you must give your speech a graphic quality not by telling a story, but by painting word pictures that allow your audience's own imagination to take over.

Specific detail allows an audience to see the scenes you are describing. This means avoiding vague references to *food* and replacing them with *pizzas* or *kebabs*. To say a meal was *delicious* merely tells them you enjoyed it. Use adjectives that conjure up specific images and trigger the senses: a *spicy* curry, a *fruity* jelly, a *savoury* pudding.

The best writers of popular fiction know they must paint word pictures. This comes from *Fallen Curtain* by Ruth Rendell:

I loved visiting gran's. Tea was lovely, fish and chips that gran didn't fetch from the shop but cooked herself, cream meringues and chocolate eclairs, tinned peaches with evaporated milk, the lot washed down with fizzy lemonade.

Can't you just feel that gassy pop getting up your nose?

The best way to learn to speak in this way is to visualise the scene you are describing. Be a film director, and tell them exactly what you see as the camera pans around the room, zooming in here and there. People will appreciate such descriptions because it is what they are used to.

Use imagery when you crack a joke too. Don't tell the gag, paint it:

> Soon after we met, Dave invited me to his eighteenth birthday party and he gave me details of his address and how to get there. He said, 'A number 8 bus will bring you right to my door – 117 Alma Road. Walk up to the front door and press the doorbell with your elbow.' 'Why my elbow?' I asked. 'Because you'll have the wine in one hand and my prezzie in the other, won't you?'

One mental picture is worth a thousand words.

USING FIGURATIVE LANGUAGE

Try to make your speech colourful and original. Similes and metaphors are particularly useful. A **simile** is a figure of speech, usually introduced by *like* or *as*, that **compares** one thing to another:

She was simmering *like* a corked volcano.
I am as awkward *as* a cow on ice.

Because a simile's function is comparison, it is not as evocative as a metaphor. A **metaphor** does not so much compare as **transform** one thing into another:

Adam had laid out four squadrons of flowers that sprouted, mute and soldierly, exactly where he had planted them.

Metaphor is more subtle and more revealing than simile, stimulating imagery beyond the original transformation. Adam's squadrons of flowers suggest something about Adam himself, evoking military associations and the sense that he is used to getting what he wants.

The right metaphor can really lift a wedding speech. Take a look at this example:

Marriage. Ever since humans gathered together in caves they – we –have displayed a basic instinct for becoming couples. Your man and your woman. Your Romeo and your Juliet. Your ying and your yang. It's as natural as his and hers bath towels. If the life of humankind were music they would all be duets. It's been a bit of a musical day one way and another. Violins in harmony with cellos. Carol in harmony with Alan. The past in harmony with the future. And, as the Bard of Avon put it: 'If music be the food of love, play on'.

And how about this?

With the two of us it is just as it is with the honeysuckle that attaches itself to the hazel tree: when it has wound and attached itself around the trunk, the two can survive together; but if someone tries to separate them, the hazel dies quickly and the honeysuckle with it. Sweet love, so it is with us: you cannot live without me, nor I without you.

That was said by Marie de France over 800 years ago – and it works just as well today. The past in harmony with the present.

Another useful figure of speech is **hyperbole**, or deliberately overstating your argument:

I've told you millions of times not to exaggerate.

In a wedding speech you can get away with saying things that most people would find embarrassing and even crass in everyday conversation:

You are the best parents/son/daughter in the world.

Not only can you get away with it – such bizarre overstatement can be highly effective, bringing a lump to the throat and a tear to the eye:

I'll love you till the ocean is folded and hung up to dry, and the seven stars go squawking like geese about the sky.

ENGAGING ALL THE SENSES

Sensory details bring breadth and depth to your descriptions. Again, we can learn a lot from writers of popular fiction. This is how Stephen King brought a character to life in *Carrie*:

> Norma led them around the dance floor to their table. She exuded odours of Avon soap, Woolworth's perfume and Juicy Fruit gum.

I bet you can see Norma. Your vision of her may be different from mine but she's there all the same, and that's all that matters. And how about this from Katherine Mansfield:

> Alexander and his friend in a train. Spring . . . wet lilac . . . spouting rain.

So few words yet the wetness is palpable.

In her autobiography, *Walled Gardens*, Annabel Davis-Doff shows how a scent can bring back memories of childhood:

> Recently, my mother and I were visiting my brother at his house near Dublin and walking through his tiny greenhouse. I reached out to a tomato plant and nipped a shoot between my thumbnail and first finger, the way my father did to prune out the small redundant leafy growths which sprout between the main trunk and branches of the plant. Without showing it to her, I held the strong-smelling leaves close to my mother's face.

> 'What does that remind you of?' I asked.

'Grenville,' she said, without a moment's pause or any sign of surprise at my question.

It made me feel close to my mother, as though I hadn't left home so long ago or gone so far away. On a warm July afternoon in Dublin she thinks the same thing, when she catches the scent of tomato plants, that I do in my garden in Connecticut.

As you speak, try to *involve* your audience. Allow them to do far more than just listen to you. Help them to *hear*, to *see*, to *smell*, to *touch*, to *taste*. Allow them to *experience* your speech.

USING SYMBOLISM

Advertising agencies spend thousands researching symbolism. Let us see what we can learn from them.

Do you remember that TV advert for a car where a rather seductive young lady asks the driver, 'Wanna show me what it can do?'? They drive off to a beach and embrace across the red bodywork. Then cut to waves coming in and going out. The implication was clear and not very subtle: buy this car and people will want to go to bed with you.

Bah, humbug? Maybe, but it works. You'll find symbols in all adverts. And the colour red crops up a lot, but usually it's more subtle, like a red sunset to advertise a liqueur, or a bunch of red roses behind a bottle of scent. Red is warm. It is vibrant, a symbol of passion, excitement and romance. When you want to suggest these things, describe a variety of hot colours, especially red.

The seasons of the year and the weather are potent symbols too. The image of a damp autumn evening is depressing while a warm spring afternoon is associated with new life, new beginnings. Writer Henry James said the two most beautiful words in the English language are *summer afternoon* because they evoke just the right emotions. Did you notice the reference to *a warm July afternoon* in Annabel Davis-Doff's reminiscence? Make use of such powerful symbols in your speech. Go for it. Tug at the heartstrings. Touch the heart:

> I took a walk in the park this morning. Every bush, every tree trembled with the flutterings of butterflies – beautiful red butterflies. It was magnificent. Yesterday there were no butterflies in my garden. Today there are thousands. Tomorrow there will be millions.

Using words colourfully and creatively will bring the middle of your speech to life like a shot of whisky in a cup of coffee.

REMEMBERING RHYTHM

A good speech should attract and hold listeners as a magnet attracts and holds iron filings. Here are four simple techniques that can turn your words into music in an audience's ears:

♦   the rule of three

♦   parallel sentences

- alliteration

- repetition.

Let's take each in turn.

The rule of three

Three is a magic number. People love to hear speakers talk to the beat of three. The effect of three words, three phrases or three sentences is powerful and memorable:

> Marriage is the meeting of two minds . . . of two hearts . . . of two souls.

> May you be blessed with happiness that grows . . . with love that deepens . . . and with peace that endures.

> We wish you fun and excitement for today . . . hopes and dreams for tomorrow . . . and love and happiness forever.

Parallel sentences

Sentences that are parallel add a rhythmic beauty that helps an audience anticipate and follow your thoughts:

> Marriage is a celebration of love. Marriage is a celebration of life. Marriage is a celebration of joy. As you walk through life, hold hands and never let go.

Alliteration

The recurrence of sounds and syllables, usually at the beginning of words, can help create just the right mood. Your speech will become special and spellbinding:

Water your garden with friendship and faith and favour.
And then watch it grow. You deserve a garden of love.

Repetition

If there is anything that is almost guaranteed to make
an audience break out into spontaneous applause it is a
repetition of strong, emotive words:

I will love you for ever . . . and ever . . . and ever!

However, use the wrong words and it will fall flat. How does
this sound?

I will think the world of you indefinitely . . . indefinitely . . .
indefinitely!

It doesn't work, does it?

KEEPING IT FLOWING

Once you have scripted a series of beautiful, funny and
moving stories and reminiscences you will need to *link* them
to form a satisfying whole. There are a number of techniques
that can help you do this. Have you noticed how entertainers,
politicians and TV presenters move easily and unobtrusively
from one topic to another? Like them, you can make your
presentation flow smoothly and gracefully from beginning to
end by making use of a few of these simple devices:

- bridges
- triggers

- rhetorical questions

- flashbacks

- identifiers

- lists

- pauses

- physical movement

- quotations, anecdotes and jokes.

Let us briefly consider each in turn.

A **bridge** is a word that alerts an audience that you are changing direction or moving to a new thought:

And he took the job in London. *Meanwhile* other developments were taking place . . .

That was bad enough. *However*, there was even worse to come . . .

So that's how Ed met Sophie. *But* romance didn't blossom right away . . .

A **trigger** is a repetition of the same word or phrase to link one topic with another.

That was what Bill *was like* at school. Now I'll tell you what he *was like* at college . . .

A **rhetorical question** – a question which does not require an answer – is another useful device to help keep a speech flowing.

> That's what makes our marriage so happy. So what advice can I offer to the newlyweds? . . .

Some members of the audience will know both the bride and the groom very well while others may only know one of them. Asking a rhetorical question is also an excellent way of telling people something while not insulting the intelligence of those already in the know.

> What can I tell you about a man who won the school prize for economics, represented the county at hockey and passed his driving test at the sixth attempt?

You can also throw in other background facts casually and inoffensively:

> . . . and passed his driving test at the sixth attempt? Sally passed first time.

A **flashback** is a sudden shift to the past to break what seems to be a predictable narrative:

> She was born in . . .
> She went to school at . . .
> She got her first job with . . . (yawn, yawn!)

It would have been far more interesting to have provided an unexpected flashback link, such as:

Today she is the attractive, sophisticated lady you see before you. *But ten years ago* she wasn't like that ...

An **identifier** is a word or phrase that keeps cropping up throughout a speech to help tie everything together. It also reinforces the audience's group identity.

Look at *our* [not *the*] beautiful bride ...
We [not *I*] wish them well ...

A **list** is a very simple way of combining apparently unrelated stories.

I remember three occasions when Tim got into trouble at school ...

But don't rely too heavily on lists because catalogue of events soon become extremely tedious to listen to.

Pausing will show an audience that you have finished a section of your speech and are about to move on to another. This is a non-verbal link that can work very well so long as it's not overdone.

By **physically moving**, your body language can tell the audience that you are moving on to something new. If you turn to the bride, they will know you are going to talk to her, or about her.

Finally, a **quotation, anecdote** or **joke** can serve as an excellent link. Here a man-on-the-bus gag links a personal compliment about good manners with a more general observation that everyone has played their part in making this a day to remember:

> Melanie always shows good old-fashioned courtesy to her fellow human beings. A rare attribute today, I'm sure you'll agree. When she was on the bus last week she stood up to give an elderly gentleman her seat. He was so surprised he fainted. When he came round he said 'Thank you' and Melanie fainted. Well I'm delighted to say there has been absolutely no shortage of courtesy here today. Things could not have gone better . . .

You will find plenty of quotations, anecdotes and jokes that you can use in the following two chapters. What a link!

3

Weaving Quotations into Your Speech

An apt quotation about love or marriage can really lift a wedding speech. But don't overdo it; quoting people can sound pompous. Just weave in one or two appropriate lines and do it in a very casual way. If you are quoting somebody famous, make it clear that you had to look it up. Say something like:

> I am reminded of the words of Groucho Marx – reminded I should say by my wife, who looked it up last night . . .

Alternatively, you could make it clear that you are reading a short extract from a book:

> I would like to read you the first two lines of one of Linda's favourite poems . . .

If you want to quote someone less well known, don't mention him or her by name. If you do, the reaction will probably be: 'Who?' Rather, say something like:

> Someone once said that . . . or, It has been said that . . .

Unfortunately many of the best quotes about love and marriage are quite cynical, and there is absolutely no place for anything negative or sneering in a wedding speech. A very simple way to get round this is to make it very clear that any cynical quote you use most certainly does *not* apply to the happy couple:

> Someone once said that he had gone into marriage with his eyes closed – her father had closed one of them and her brother had closed the other. Well, all I can say is that William went into his marriage with his eyes wide open. And seeing how beautiful Mary looks today, who could blame him?

There are thousands of good quotations about love and marriage. I have listed some of the best below. You'll find something old, something new, something borrowed, but definitely nothing blue. However, if you can't find anything suitable, look through one or more of the books listed under 'Further Reading' at the back of this book. Alternatively, you could quote something you have heard or read that seems particularly appropriate for the occasion. If you quote a line or two from a song, make sure that it is specific enough to mean something to the bride and bridegroom, yet is still general enough to be appreciated by the rest of the audience. I recently heard a bridegroom say this, and it almost brought the house down:

> Well, Liz, in the words of your favourite Carpenters' song, 'We've only just begun. So much of life ahead. A kiss for luck [*he blew her a kiss*] and we're on our way.' Yes, Liz, we've only just begun!

Later they played the record and there wasn't a dry eye in the house.

For the less adventurous speaker, here is a sample of more conventional quotations. You'll find a happy marriage of humour and sentiment – of the ridiculous and the sublime – because that's what a good wedding speech should be all about.

LOVE AND MARRIAGE

How do I love thee? Let me count the ways.
I love thee to the depth and breadth and height
My soul can reach (Elizabeth Barrett Browning).

Love has the magic power to make a beggar a king (Emma Goldman).

My heart, thinking
'How beautiful he is',
Is like a swift river
Which though one dams it and dams it
Will still break through (Otomo no Sakano-e no Iratsume).

Know, my love, that I call you a thief because you have stolen my heart (Margaret of Nassau).

How many idiots has love made wise?
How many fools eloquent?
How many homebred squires accomplished?
How many cowards brave? (Aphra Behn).

As a highwayman knows that he must come to the gallows eventually, so a fashionably extravagant youth knows that, sooner or later, he must come to matrimony (Maria Edgeworth).

Everything which is exchanged between husband and wife in their life together can only be the free gift of love. It can never be demanded by one or the other as a right (Ellen Key).

I love you so passionately that I must hide a great part of my love not to oppress you with it (Marie de Sevigne).

When my soul was in lost-and-found
You came to claim it (Carole King in *A Natural Woman*).

Love, the strongest and deepest element in all life, the harbinger of hope, of joy, of ecstasy; love, the defier of all laws, of all conventions; love, the freest, the most powerful moulder of human destiny (Emma Goldman).

When you see what some girls marry, you realise how they must hate to work for a living (Helen Rowland).

A good marriage is one which allows for change and growth in individuals (Pearl Buck).

I've sometimes thought of marrying, and then I've thought again (Noel Coward).

Before marriage, a man will lie awake all night thinking about something you said; after marriage, he'll fall asleep before you finish saying it (Helen Rowland).

Marriage is an alliance of two people, one of whom never remembers birthdays and the other never forgets them (Ogden Nash).

In most good marriages, the woman is her husband's closest friend and adviser (Nancy Reagan).

When marrying, one should ask oneself this question: Do you believe that you will be able to converse well with this woman into your old age? (Friedrich Nietzche).

Well married, a man is winged: ill-matched, he is shackled (Henry Ward Beecher).

Marriage is like throwing yourself into the river when all you wanted was a drink (Del Boy, aka David Jason).

Marriage is like a lottery, but you can't tear up your ticket if you lose (F. M. Knowles).

Man and wife, a king and queen with one or two subjects, and a few square yards of territory of their own: this, really, is marriage. It is a true freedom because it is a true fulfilment, for man, woman and children (D. H. Lawrence).

Love appears every day
for one who offers love.
That wisdom is enough (Mechtild von Magdeburg).

I was so cold I almost got married (Shelley Winters).

Somebody loves me; How do I know?

Somebody's eyes have told me so! (Hattie Starr, popular Victorian music hall song).

There are no wrinkles in the heart (Juliette Drouet).

At one glance
I love you
With a thousand hearts (Mihri Hatun).

Do you want me to tell you something really subversive? Love is everything it's cracked up to be. That's why people are so cynical about it (Erica Jong).

Love, the quest: marriage, the conquest (Helen Rowland).

I am yours,
you are mine.
Of this we are certain.
You are lodged
in my heart,
the small key
is lost.
You must stay there forever (Frau Ava).

We grow old as soon as we cease to love and trust (Louise Honorine de Choiseul).

We can only learn to love by loving (Iris Murdoch).

Love doesn't just sit there, like a stone, it has to be made, like bread; remade all the time, made new (Ursula K. LeGuin).

If ever two were one, then surely we.
If ever man were lov'd by wife, then surely thee (Anne Bradstreet).

These three efforts are the golden threads with which domestic happiness is woven: to repress a harsh answer, to confess a fault, and to stop (right or wrong) in the midst of argument (Caroline Gilman).

I'll venture to say, few, if any, in a married state, ever lived in sweeter harmony than we did (Elizabeth Haddon Estaugh).

Love is a general leveller – it makes a king a slave: and inspires the slave with every joy a prince can taste (Elizabeth Inchbald).

The most vital right is the right to love and to be loved (Emma Goldman).

A marriage where not only esteem, but passion is kept awake, is, I am convinced, the most perfect state of happiness: but it requires great care to keep this tender plant alive (Frances Brooke).

Two pure souls fused into one by an impassioned love – friends, counsellors – a mutual support and inspiration to each other amid life's struggles, must know the highest human happiness. This is marriage; and it is the only corner-stone of an enduring home (Elizabeth Cady Stanton).

Partnership, not dependence, is the real romance in marriage (Muriel Fox).

It usually takes some time for the husband and wife to know each other's humours and habits, and to find out what surrender of their own they can make with the least reluctance for their mutual good (Amelia Opie).

I love and the world is mine! (Florence Earle Coates).

There are only two things that are absolute realities, love and knowledge, and you can't escape them (Ella Wheeler Wilcox).

For 'twas not into my ear you whispered but into my heart. 'Twas not my lips you kissed, but my soul (Judy Garland in *My Soul is Lost*).

Blossoms crowd the branches: too beautiful to endure. Thinking of you, I break into bloom again (Hsueh T'ao).

I'd rather marry a wise old man than a young fool (Anna Maria of Braunscheig).

Love is moral even without marriage, but marriage is immoral without love (Ellen Key).

Love is a mighty god, you know,
That rules with potent sway;
And when he draws his awful bow,
We mortals must obey (Mary Masters).

It is a truth universally acknowledged, that a single man in possession of good fortune, must be in want of a wife (Jane Austen, opening words of *Pride and Prejudice*).

Love and hope are twins (Maria Brooks).

I sometimes think the gods have united human beings by some mysterious principle, as musical notes become chords. Or is it that the souls originally one have been divided, and each seeks the half it lost? (Lydia M. Child).

Love understands love; it needs no talk (Frances Ridley Havergal).

Love is life, love is the lamp that lights the universe: without that light this goodly frame the earth, is a barren promontory and man the quintessence of dust (Mary Elizabeth Braddon).

Love remoulds the world nearer to the heart's desire (Mary Berenson).

If love does not know how to give and take without restrictions, it is not love, but a transaction that never fails to lay stress on a plus and a minus (Emma Goldman).

Youth's for an hour,
Beauty's a flower.
But love is the jewel that wins the world (Moira O'Neill).

There is only one happiness in life, to love and be loved (George Sand).

Love is not getting, but giving. It is sacrifice. And sacrifice is glorious! (Marie Dressier).

The sight of you is as necessary for me as the sun for spring flowers (Marguerite of Valois).

Dawn love is silver,
Wait for the west:
Old love is gold love –
Old love is best (Katherine Lee Bates).

Whoever loves true life, will love true love (Elizabeth Barrett Browning).

There is no more lovely, friendly and charming relationship, communion or company than a good marriage (Martin Luther).

Love is the light and sunshine of life. We cannot fully enjoy ourselves, or anything else, unless someone we love enjoys it with us (Sir John Avebury).

Love is the wine of existence (Henry Ward Beecher).

The great secret of successful marriage is to treat all disasters as incidents and none of the incidents as disasters (Harold Nicolson).

Love is a great force in life; it is indeed the greatest of all things (E.M. Forster).

Eternal love, and everlasting love (Thomas Otway).

Love is more than gold or great riches (John Lydgate).

Love is the only weapon we need (Revd. H.R.L. Sheppard).

When one loves somebody everything is clear – where to go, what to do – it all takes care of itself and one doesn't have to ask anybody about anything (Maxim Gorky).

Of all forms of caution, caution in love is perhaps the most fatal to true happiness (Bertrand Russell).

To fear love is to fear life, and those who fear life are already three parts dead (Bertrand Russell).

Success in marriage is more than *finding* the right person; it is *being* the right person (Rabbi B.R. Bricker).

Marriage is a mutual partnership if both parties know when to be mute (Anon).

I love you more than yesterday and less than tomorrow (Edmond Rostand).

A toast to sweethearts. May all sweethearts become married couples and may all married couples remain sweethearts (Anon).

Marriage halves our griefs, doubles our joys, and quadruples our expenses (Vincent Lean).

The love we give away is the only love we keep (Elbert Hubbard).

The trouble was, I went into marriage with both eyes closed – her father closed one and her brother closed the other (Max Kauffman).

Love doesn't make the world go round. Love is what makes the ride worthwhile (Franklin P. Jones).

A successful marriage is an edifice that must be rebuilt every day (André Maurois).

A marriage is a long conversation which always seems too short (André Maurois).

A successful marriage involves falling in love many times – with the same person (Bob Monkhouse).

Husbands are like fires . . . they go out when unattended (Zsa Zsa Gabor).

Marriage is a great institution – no family should be without it (Bob Hope).

Love is like oxygen. You get too much you get so high — not enough you're going to die (D. Ream's Peter Cunnah).

You can always tell when a husband is lying – his lips move (Ken Livingstone).

How absurd and delicious it is to fall in love with somebody younger than yourself (Barbara Pym).

The critical period in matrimony is breakfast time (A.P. Herbert).

Never go to bed mad. Stay up and fight (Phyllis Diller).

When a man brings his wife flowers for no reason – there's a reason (Molly McGee).

Love makes the world go around (Proverb).

Whenever you're wrong, admit it; whenever you're right, shut up (Ogden Nash).

The reason husbands and wives do not understand each other is because they belong to different sexes (Dorothy Dix).

True love never grows old (Proverb).

Like fingerprints, all marriages are different (George Bernard Shaw).

Marriage is so popular because it combines the maximum of temptation with the maximum of opportunity (George Bernard Shaw).

Love does not consist of gazing at each other but in looking outward together in the same direction (Antoine de Saint-Exupéry).

Marriage is like holding an electric wire – it can be shocking but you can't let go (Anon).

Their love makes Vesuvius look like a damp sparkler (Alida Baxter).

Don't marry anyone until you've seen them drunk (Anon).

Where love is concerned, too much is not enough (Anon).

Any man who says he can see through a woman is missing a lot (Groucho Marx).

All unhappy marriages come from the husband having brains (P.G. Wodehouse).

Marriage is like pleading guilty with an indefinite sentence and no parole (Horace Rumpole, with a little help from John Mortimer).

For in what stupid age or nation,
Was marriage ever out of fashion? (Samuel Butler).

Don't let your marriage go stale. Change the bag on the Hoover of life (Victoria Wood).

Marriage is the only adventure open to the cowardly (Voltaire).

Why does a woman work ten years to change a man's habits and then complain that he's not the man she married? (Barbra Streisand).

It has been said that a bride's attitude towards her betrothed can be summed up by three words associated with weddings: Aisle, altar, hymn (Anon).

Her husband made her happy by adding some magic to their marriage . . . he disappeared (Nicholas Murray Butler).

When a girl marries she exchanges the attentions of many men for the inattention of one (Helen Rowland).

You live in your heart, so you have to be very careful about what you put there (Marti Caine).

A daughter's a daughter for all of her life, but a son is a son till he gets a wife (Anon).

In the arithmetic of love, one plus one equals everything and two minus one equals nothing (Mignon McLaughlin).

Two can live as cheaply as one, and after marriage they do (Anon).

Nowadays two can live as cheaply as one large family used to (Joey Adams).

A happy marriage is the union of two good forgivers (Robert Quillen).

True love is like the misty rain that falls so softly, yet floods the river (Nigerian proverb).

Marriage teaches you loyalty, forbearance, self-restraint and many other qualities you wouldn't need if you stayed single (Anon).

A ring on the finger is worth two on the phone (Harold Thomson).

Two souls with but a single thought,
Two hearts that beat as one (Maria Lovell).

Marriage is our last, best chance to grow up (Joseph Barth).

Let there be spaces in your togetherness (Kahlil Gibran).

When you are in love, you tell each other a thousand things without talking (Hawaiian proverb).

Let's get married . . . It's a piece of paper but it says, 'I love you' (The Proclaimers, *Let's Get Married*).

I will never marry because I could never be satisfied with any woman stupid enough to have me (Abraham Lincoln).

If you would have a happy family life, remember two things: in matters of principle, stand like a rock; in matters of taste, swim with the current (Thomas Jefferson).

The heart can do anything (French proverb).

A good husband should be deaf and a good wife blind (French proverb).

Some people ask the secret of our long marriage. We take time to go out to a restaurant two times a week. A little candlelight, dinner, soft music and dancing. She goes Tuesday, I go Fridays (Henry Youngman).

It takes two to make a marriage a success and only one a failure (Herbert Samuel).

Don't let's ask for the moon. We have the stars! (Bette Davis to Paul Henreid in *Now Voyager*).

Married couples resemble a pair of scissors, often moving in opposite directions, yet always punishing anyone who comes between them (Sydney Smith).

Every man needs a wife because things sometimes go wrong that you can't blame on the government (Anon).

Like the measles, love is most dangerous when it comes late in life (Lord Byron).

Actually, I believe in marriage, having done it several times (Joan Collins).

Second marriage: the triumph of hope over experience (Samuel Johnson).

Zsa Zsa Gabor got married as a one-off and it was so successful she turned it into a series (Bob Hope).

I'm not so old, and not so plain, and I'm quite prepared to marry again (W.S. Gilbert – useful for second marriages).

Love and marriage,
Love and marriage,
Go together like a horse and carriage. (Popular song by Sammy Cahn – particularly apt if the couple travelled by horse and carriage).

Marriage is an armed alliance against the outside world (G.K. Chesterton).

The most beautiful things in the world cannot be seen or even touched. They must be felt with the heart (Helen Keller).

Everything I do I do it for you (Record-breaking No. 1 hit by Bryan Adams).

Love is like a curry. You really have to have confidence in it to enjoy it (Mike Smith).

A woman is like a tea bag – you don't know her strength until she is in hot water (Nancy Reagan).

Mary and I have been married for 47 years, and not once have we ever had an argument serious enough to mention the word divorce . . . murder, yes, but divorce, never (Jack Benny).

I belong to Bridegrooms Anonymous. Whenever I feel like getting married they send over a lady in a housecoat and hair curlers to burn my toast for me (Dick Martin).

I am feeling very lonely. I've been married for 15 years, and yesterday my wife ran off with the chap next door. I'm going to miss him terribly (Les Dawson).

I don't for the life of me understand why people keep insisting marriage is doomed. All five of mine worked out (Peter De Vries).

I'm the only man who has a marriage licence made out 'To Whom It May Concern' (Mickey Rooney).

Marriage turns a night owl into a homing pigeon (Glenn Shelton).

Most girls seem to marry men who happen to be like their fathers. Maybe that's why so many mothers cry at weddings (Jenny Eclair).

Marriage is like wine. It gets better with age (Dudley Moore).

Love is the answer and you know that for sure (John Lennon).

When I proposed, I said, 'I offer you my hand, my heart and my washing' (A.A. Milne).

Marriage: a strong union which defies management (Will Rogers).

It was a beautiful wedding – one of my better ones (Jim Davidson).

Woman begins by resisting man's advances and ends by blocking his retreat (Oscar Wilde).

I never married because there was no need. I have three pets at home which answer the same purpose as a husband. I have a dog which growls every morning, a parrot which swears all the afternoon and a cat that comes home late at night (Marie Corelli).

Getting married is like getting a dog. It teaches you to be less self-centred, to expect sudden, surprising outbursts of affection, and not to be upset by a few scratches on your car (Will Stanton).

Love is like quicksilver in the hand. Leave the fingers open and it stays; clutch it, and it darts away (Dorothy Parker).

Laugh and the world laughs with you, snore and you sleep alone (Anthony Burgess).

4

Saying it with Humour

A humorous anecdote (short personal story) or a joke can make a speech individual and memorable. Choose your material very carefully. It must be in keeping with your own personality, the tone of your speech and the expectations of your audience. It must also be original. Don't repeat any story or joke which you recently heard on television because Murphy's Law tells us that at least one other person in the room will have been watching the same programme. Similarly, don't tell one that has already been aired at a previous family gathering. Finally, don't get carried away – you are not a stand-up comedian.

TESTING YOUR MATERIAL

Never use any material unless you are sure it complies with the 3R rule of story-telling. A joke or anecdote must be:

♦ Relevant

♦ Realistic

♦ Retellable.

Relevant

Your story must be *meaningful* to your audience. You may know a wonderful gag about a window cleaner and an MP. Even if it is the funniest story in the world, don't tell it unless the bride, groom or best man is a window cleaner, or an MP. In this chapter you will find several anecdotes and jokes about various jobs and hobbies. You will also find some good jokes and lines that would be particularly useful in each of the main speeches.

Realistic

Your story doesn't have to be true, but it should sound as it if *could* be true. Reg Smythe, the cartoonist responsible for the long-running *Andy Capp* strip, used to say, 'Never draw anything that hasn't happened or couldn't happen.' The same principle applies to making a speech: you should never talk about anything that hasn't happened or couldn't happen. So it is fine to talk about a man with three hats, but not about a man with three heads.

Retellable

'Something old, something new, something borrowed, something blue.' That is what a bride is supposed to have about her on her wedding day. The first three things – something old, something new and something borrowed – also apply to the contents of a good speech. The fourth – something blue – most certainly does *not.*

GETTING IT RIGHT

Aim to be amusing but not *too* risqué. A little flippancy is fine but don't say anything offensive or cynical. To say, 'Marriage isn't a word, it's a sentence' is a great line for a stand-up comedian but not for a wedding speech. This is the bride's day and no one should say a word against her or the institution of marriage. So while a little crack about her job or hobby is fine, there must be absolutely no reference to sex, or any previous relationships. Also, try to include a joke or two against yourself. Audiences love speakers who don't take themselves too seriously. Before you tell a story or crack a joke, ask yourself whether it passes this test which the late and great Bob Monkhouse devised for all his potential material:

1.   Do *you* think it is funny?

2.   Can you say it confidently and with comfort?

3.   Is there any danger of offending anyone?

4.   Will they understand and appreciate it?

Do *you* think it is funny?

If you're not really happy about a joke or story you will not tell it confidently. Not only that, your audience probably won't find it funny either. Professional gagsters follow this maxim: If in doubt, leave it out. So should you.

Can you say it confidently and with comfort?

Stick to the KISS principle: Keep It Short and Simple. Avoid any long or complicated stories, difficult words or phrases and anything requiring regional or national accents. And ask yourself: Is this story right for *me*? A twenty-year-old should not tell a story about his silver wedding anniversary.

Is there any danger of offending anyone?

Avoid anything racist, sexist or ageist, and steer well clear of politics, religion, sex and disabilities. In short, use your common sense. Remember: If in doubt, leave it out.

Will they understand and appreciate it?

Your audience may be aged anything between 3 and 93 and they will probably have a very wide range of backgrounds. So it is impossible to give a speech totally suited to everyone present. However, what you can do is avoid the extremes of, on the one hand, telling childish jokes and, on the other hand, telling complicated, technical stories comprehensible only to a professor of applied nuclear physics. Also avoid in-jokes; they are a real turn-off for those not in the know. Finally, remember that some jokes which are really funny when *read*, can be totally incomprehensible when *heard*. This can be illustrated by the following:

> Chris isn't a great reader so I was surprised to find a tattered volume of an out-of-date encyclopaedia in his room. When I saw the letters on the side of the volume I laughed at the thought of what must have been his utter surprise and shattering disappointment when he first got the book home. The letters read: 'HOW to HUG'.

You can *see* how this amusing confusion was caused, but you would not have easily appreciated it if you had *heard* the gag. (Its punchline: 'The letters read: H-O-W to H-U-G' would have sounded like double Dutch to you.) So the moral is clear: always rehearse your speech *out loud*, preferably in front of a small audience or on videotape. Then if something doesn't work – as this one certainly wouldn't have – take it out.

ADAPTING AND PERSONALISING MATERIAL

Once you are satisfied that a joke or anecdote passes the 3R test of storytelling and the Monkhouse Test, you will need to adapt it, that is make a few changes here and there until it is *meaningful* to your audience. For example, if you want to tell a story about a taxi driver you might well be able to adapt one about a bus driver or a lorry driver. Any gag involving motor vehicles or a long road journey could probably apply to any of them.

Then you must personalise your material. Don't tell a story about a taxi driver – any old taxi driver – tell one about a particular taxi driver, probably about the bride, the bridegroom, the best man or you. Don't talk about 'a town', mention *your* town. And don't say 'he drove down a back street', say 'Vikram drove down Inkerman Street'. In other words, give your audience enough local details so they can actually see the events as you describe them – if only in their mind's eye.

Being positively insulting

Funnily enough, a teasing little joke and a sincere compliment often fit in very well together. For example:

> Helen recently joined the string section of the town orchestra. She practises at home day and night. She's always harping on about something or other [*pause*]. Well, angels do, don't they?

Here's another example:

When I asked Ian about all the wedding arrangements he said, 'Oh, I'll leave all that to you. But I do want Bells – and at least three cases of it' [*pause*]. Well I don't know about Bells, but I work with Ian at Grange Hill Comprehensive – and I can tell you that he is certainly one of the best Teachers I know.

So try to sugar your jokes with praise.

TIMING YOUR DELIVERY

You will have noticed that I have suggested where you pause to get your laughs. Usually this is obvious. It's all about timing. If the guests clap or cheer (even if you weren't expecting it), pause. If you tell a serious or sentimental story, pause for a second or two to let the moral sink in. However, if a joke falls flat, as soon as you realise it get straight on – make it seem as if no laughs were expected. Never, never repeat a joke or punchline, or say anything like 'You're slow today', or 'Don't you get it?' – that makes it look like you are begging for a positive reaction. If it's funny they'll laugh, if it's not they won't.

Right, here are some anecdotes and jokes about various jobs and hobbies, followed by some more general little stories, gags and other lines particularly suited to each of the main speeches. Choose one or two relevant ones, adapt and personalise them, and tell them using your own words. Or, better still, try to think of original ones yourself. If they happen to be true, or at least are based on truth, then so much the better.

JOKES ABOUT JOBS

Some stories and gags could apply to *any* job, for example:

Dave's boss says he's a miracle worker . . . It's a miracle if he works.

I asked Sue how many people work at her company. 'About a half,' she replied.

Jamie has a perfect attendance record . . . He's never missed a tea break.

Poor old Stuart. Off sick again all last week . . . this time with a broken thermos flask.

Andy asked me to give his application form a quick once over before he sent it off. It was a good thing he did. Where he was asked: 'Length of residence at current address' he had replied, 'About 20 metres – not counting the garage.'

On Ryan's first day at his new job, the manager greeted him with a warm handshake and a smile, and then he gave him a broom. He said, 'Son, your first job is to sweep up'. 'But I'm a college graduate,' Ryan replied indignantly. 'Oh, I'm sorry. I didn't realise that,' said the manager. 'Here, give me the broom . . . I'll show you how.'

When Andy left his last job, they gave him this reference: 'Any employer who gets Mr Capp to work for him will be very lucky.'

However, it is far better if you refer to someone's actual job and to the name of the company they work for.

With a little thought, many of the following gags can be adapted for other occupations as well.

Architect/draughtsman
Every morning, as Tom leaves for work he says, 'Ah, well, back to the drawing board.'

Builder/electrician/handyman/plumber
You all know Dean is a builder, but what you probably don't know is that he's also a great story-teller. When he tells a customer that he'll be there at 8, he will be more likely to turn up at 10. Anyway, today he is going to give us a speech and that will be the first time he has ever finished something on the same day that he started it.

Building site/factory employee
When Shaun was interviewed for his job, his supervisor asked him if he could make tea. Shaun said, 'Yes.' 'And can you drive a fork lift truck?' his boss continued. 'Why?' asked Shaun, 'How big is the teapot?'

Bus driver/taxi driver
A woman asked Terry whether he stopped/could stop at the Ritz (or some local expensive hotel). 'No, madam, not on my wages,' he replied.

Buyer/contracts officer/negotiator
Stephen would never accept a bribe. One day he was offered a Porsche. He was indignant, 'I cannot accept a gift like that,' he fumed. 'I quite understand,' replied the would-be briber, 'I tell you what, why don't I sell it to you for a fiver?' Stephen thought about it for a moment and said, 'In that case, I'll take two.'

Car dealer
Arthur pointed to an old Mondeo. 'I can't shift this,' he said, 'I'll have to reduce it.' 'By how much?' I asked. 'Oh, by about three owners and 50,000 miles,' he replied.

Carpenter
Do you know how Jim decides whether to use a nail or screw when doing his carpentry? I'll tell you. He hammers a nail in and if the wood splits he knows he should have used a screw.

Chemist/pharmacist
Have you noticed the signs at Robin's pharmacy? One says: 'We dispense with accuracy' and the other says, 'Try our new cough medicine . . . You'll never get any better.'

Church
Dominic announced to the congregation: 'Sunday's sermon will be entitled "What is hell?" Come early and listen to our choir.'

Civil servant
Why don't Civil Servants stare out of the window in the morning? If they did, they'd have nothing to do in the afternoon.

Cleaner/housekeeper
Not long after Hilda had begun working for Shiners, her office manager made a spot check of her work. 'Look at this desk!' he exclaimed, 'it hasn't been cleaned for over a month.' 'Don't blame me,' Hilda replied, 'I've only worked here for a fortnight.'

Dentist/doctor
Bill was working on a female patient's teeth when he suddenly looked at his watch and asked her to scream loudly. She did so and then enquired whether that was part of her treatment. 'Oh no,' said Bill, 'I've got a train to catch in half an hour and my waiting room is absolutely packed.'

DSS worker
Jimmy told me about a lady who asked if something could be done for her. 'I've got no clothes,' she said, 'and the vicar visits me three times a week.'

Electrical repairs/ other repairs job
An elderly gent went into Rob's Repairs. 'I brought my computer in to get it fixed back in 1995 but then the Old Bill paid me a visit and – well, I only got out this morning,' he explained, handing Rob a crumbled old ticket. Rob went into the back room and was gone ages. He returned and handed the ticket back to the old man, saying, 'We should have it ready by next Friday, sir.'

Electrician
A woman phoned Jimmy and asked why he hadn't called to repair her doorbell, as agreed. 'I did call', Jimmy protested. 'I rang three times and got no answer so I thought you must be out.'

Estate agent/traffic warden/ any other 'unpopular' occupation
Ninety-nine per cent of estate agents give the rest a bad name.

Farmer

Joe was having problems with walkers crossing his land. So he put up a notice on one of his gates: 'Trespassers admitted free. The bull charges later.'

Hairdresser/barber

Definition of a hairdresser: someone who always talks behind their customers' backs.

Insurance office employee

Jim says people write some very strange things on their insurance claim forms. Here are a couple he told me about: 'The man was all over the place on the road – I had to swerve several times before I hit him.' And here's another: 'I was thrown out of my car and was found in a ditch by some cows.'

IT

A computer programmer had been missing for a week. Finally, someone noticed and the police were notified. They broke down his front door and found him dead in the shower, an empty family size bottle of shampoo at his side. The programmer appeared to have died from a combination of exposure and exhaustion. The puzzle was explained when the police read the instructions on the shampoo bottle: 'Wet hair. Apply shampoo. Repeat.'

Librarian/book shop employee

A man asked Sarah, 'Have you a book entitled *Man, Master of the Home*?' She looked at him in disbelief for a moment and then replied, 'Try the Fiction section.'

Lorry driver/HGV driver

Alec was driving down a country lane when he met an on-coming lorry. Neither driver was willing to give way. After what seemed like an eternity, the other driver reached for a book, sat back and started to read. Alec got out of his cab, marched purposefully towards the other vehicle, tapped on the window and said, 'Excuse me, mate, can I borrow that book once you've finished it?'

Nurse

At the wedding rehearsal, when Dougal held out the ring, Florence took his pulse.

Police officer/traffic warden/AA/RAC

A motorist pulled up at the Coldra Junction and asked Jeremy whether it mattered whether he took the A48 or M4 to Cardiff. 'No, not to me, it doesn't,' Jeremy replied.

Public house/brewery/off-licence employee

Jack loves his work at the 5-X brewery. In fact, he often takes his work home with him.

Railway/bus company employee

A man said he wanted to catch the late train to Manchester. 'Take the 11.15,' Richard suggested. 'That's usually as late as any.'

Salesperson

John's boss says he's the most independent salesman he has ever employed . . . he doesn't take orders from anyone.

Shop-keeper

Have you seen the sign in Mark's shop window? It says: 'Don't go elsewhere to be cheated. Come in here.' And what about the sign inside? It says: 'Our boast is that we never allow a dissatisfied customer to leave this shop'.

Solicitor/management accountant

I dreamt that Horace died and went to the gates of heaven where he was to be interviewed by St Peter to see if he should be let into heaven or sent down to hell. 'I don't know why I died so young,' complained Horace, 'it doesn't seem fair, I'm only 31.' 'I know,' replied St Peter, 'but according to all the time you've billed your clients for, you're at least 190.'

Teacher/lecturer

A little lad at the back stood up and asked, 'Sir, can I be punished for something I haven't done?' 'Of course not,' Ben replied. 'That's good,' said the boy, 'because I haven't done my homework.'

HUMOUR ABOUT HOBBIES

A gag or one-liner about someone's hobby or interest is also certain to go down well. Here is a selection of possibilities.

Amateur boxing/judo/karate

David is a very colourful fighter . . . he always comes home black and blue.

Amateur dramatics

I remember the day Steve came home and told me he'd got his first part. 'I play a man who's been married for 25 years,' he announced. 'That's a great start, son,' I said. 'Just keep at it and one of these days you'll get a speaking part.'

Book collecting

Nicholas is so proud of his book collection. Last week he complained to me that he now has so many that he just doesn't know what to do with them. I suggested that he tried reading them.

Cats/any other pet

Stefan's cat is brilliant. I asked her what two minus two was and she said nothing.

CD collecting

Adam has a magnificent CD collection. One day he went into a record shop and asked for the Beatles' *White Album* but the girl said they hadn't got it. 'Well would you mind taking another look?' he asked. 'Perhaps you have it in some other colour.'

Cinema/theatre/bingo

Harrison left in the middle of the film and trod on the foot of the woman at the end of the row. When he returned, he said, 'Did I stand on your foot on my way out?' 'Yes,' she replied. 'Good,' he said, 'then this is the right row.'

Cooking

Sally's cooking melts in your mouth. I wish she'd defrost it first.

Crosswords

The smallest things seem to bother Jane. Last week she was

doing a crossword puzzle and she asked me, 'What is a female sheep?' I said 'Ewe' and she burst into tears.

Dancing/badminton
Steve met Emma at a club and during their first dance he stood on her feet several times. As she limped back to her seat, he apologised, saying, 'I'm a little stiff from badminton.' She replied, 'I don't care where you're from. Keep off my bloody feet.'

DIY
Ray was doing some decorating, so he got out his step-ladder. I don't think he gets on too well with his real ladder.

Dogs
Keith told me his dog, Fido, is just like one of the family. I'm still trying to work out which one.

Driving
When Sanjay got home from work he was greeted by Vicki. She told him she had some good news and some bad news about their brand new top-of-the-range car. Sanjay said, 'Okay, what's the good news?' And Vicki replied, 'The air bag works.'

Fitness
Adam met his new personal trainer and was asked what he hoped to achieve over the next couple of months. 'I've always wanted to do the splits,' Adam explained. 'That should be possible,' his trainer said, 'how flexible are you?' 'Oh, I'm very flexible' Adam replied, 'I can get here most Mondays, Wednesdays or Fridays.'

Fitness (or lack of it)

My doctor told me that exercise could add years to my life. He was right. I feel ten years older already.

Football (playing)

Wayne's team were getting hammered last Saturday. He went up to the referee and said, 'Can we have a new ball?' 'What's wrong with the one you have?' the ref asked. And Wayne replied, 'The other team are always playing with it.'

Football (watching)

My doctor told me I should avoid any unnecessary excitement so I started supporting (*groom's favourite team*).

Fashion

As you know, Alicia is really into fashion. She just told me the latest hot news and, Darren, you would be wise to take careful note of it. Next year there will be absolutely no change in pockets.

Fishing

The only time a fisherman tells the truth is when he calls another fisherman a liar.

Gambling/Lotto

Terry told me he dreamt he'd won a million on the Lottery. June said to him, 'What shall we do about all those begging letters?' And Terry replied, 'We'll just keep sending them.'

Golf

After a long and frustrating day on the course, Nick turned angrily on his caddie, 'You know, you must be the worst caddie in the world!' 'I don't think so,' replied his caddie. 'That would be too much of a coincidence.'

Hiking/walking
Ian had hoped to climb Ben Nevis during his holiday, but he didn't get any farther than Fort William . . . it took him five days to walk there and two more to refold the map.

Hitch-hiking
Ford always begins his hitch-hiking at 3 in the morning. He says it's the best time to miss the traffic.

Motorbike trials/racing car trials/sheep dog trials
I went with Phil to last year's Scottish sheepdog trials. 31 were found guilty.

Musician
Simon asked his music teacher for her honest opinion about his compositions. She looked at him straight in the eye and said, 'I believe your songs will be played when Beethoven and the Beatles are forgotten . . . but not before.'

Poker
Billy used to really love our Saturday evening card schools. But I remember one night when he jumped up from the table, white with rage. 'Stop the game!' he yelled. 'Steve's cheating!' 'How do you know?' I asked. And Billy replied, 'Because he's not playing the hand I dealt him.'

Pony club/gymkhana/ horse riding
Lucinda called her pony Radish and went round telling everyone, 'This is my horse Radish.'

Pop group
Elton says they're going to change the name of their band to Free Beer. Great name, isn't it? Think of how it will look on pub notice boards. The punters will pile in.

Reading
George asked the librarian if she could suggest a good book – something quite deep. She replied, 'How about *20,000 Leagues Under the Sea?*'

Retail therapy
What's the most expensive vehicle, per mile, to operate? A shopping trolley.

Skiing
Like Eddie, I thought of taking up skiing ... but I let it slide.

Television
I'm so looking forward to coming home, opening a beer, sitting on the sofa and watching Paula's favourite television programmes.

Water skiing
Adrian got a pair of water skis for Christmas. He spent the next six months looking for a lake on a slope.

WEDDING SPEECH ONE-LINERS
Any of the quotations, jokes and stories given so far can be adapted and personalised for any wedding speech. However, here are some lines which are likely to be particularly useful for each of the main speeches.

For the bride's father

Ladies and Gentlemen, it has been said that love is the light and sunshine of life. We cannot enjoy ourselves, or anything else, unless someone we love enjoys it with us. Well from this day forth Mavis and Derek will be enjoying their lives together ... [Or some other appropriate quotation hook].

I haven't lost a daughter, I've gained an overdraft.

I'm not losing a daughter; I'm gaining a bathroom.

Janet pleased me by laughing uproariously when reading the draft of this little speech, only to inform me that it was my spelling that so amused her.

A man took his wife along to a marriage counsellor. The counsellor asked him to explain their problem. The man said, 'What's 'er name here claims I don't pay her enough attention.'

You know the honeymoon's over when the groom stops helping his wife with the dishes – and starts doing them himself.

Being a romantic sort of girl, Edwina insisted on getting married in her grandmother's dress. She looked absolutely fabulous – but her poor granny nearly froze to death.

I'll never forget my wedding day. You never saw two happier people than her mother and father.

A good marriage lasts for ever. A bad one just seems to.

I told my wife that I don't believe in combining marriage and a career – which is why I haven't worked since my wedding day.

Nice to see you all dressed up in those dicky bows. Are you here for the snooker?

Today I gave away my daughter ... and you will never believe the pleasure that gave me.

Always remember that money comes first and last. You've got to make it first and then make it last.

I asked my wife if she remembered our wedding night. 'Steve,' she said, 'that was 27 years ago, there's no need to apologise now.'

I shall never forget my marriage because I had to ask my wife's mother permission to marry her daughter. 'Have you the means to make her happy?' she asked. 'Well,' I said, 'it'll make her laugh and I'm afraid that's the best I can do.'

Try praising your wife, even if it does frighten her at first.

When Tony asked me for Cherie's hand in marriage, I asked, 'Tony, do you think you're earning enough to support a family?' 'Yes,' he replied. 'Think very carefully now,' I added, 'after all you know there are six of us.' Only joking Tony. But I do want you to know you really are one of the family now ...

Hamish asked me if I thought he was old enough to marry Carrie. 'Oh yes,' I replied, 'because you'll age fast enough.'

When we got married my wife didn't have a rag on her back. But she's got plenty of them now.

I read that marriage was going out of fashion. Well, if that's true, have you ever seen two people looking so happy to be out of fashion?

I can still hear my bride-to-be saying to her mother, 'Mum, I've still got so much to do and I want everything to be perfect. I'm determined not to overlook even the most insignificant detail.' And her mother replying, 'Don't worry, I'll make sure your father's there.'

After we'd been married for about a month, one evening I asked, 'You don't mind if I point out a few of your faults, do you?' 'Not at all,' she replied, 'it's those little faults that stopped me from getting a better husband.'

Sometimes Liz is a little economical with the truth. But, to be fair to her, that's the only thing she's economical with.

Zoë admits that she does have some faults, but she insists that ever being wrong isn't one of them.

On the sea of matrimony you have to expect occasional squalls.

Indira never loses her temper, but occasionally she mislays it.

Any man who thinks he is smarter than his wife is married to a very smart woman.

A few weeks after we got married I came home from work to find Emma in tears. 'I feel terrible,' she said. 'When I was pressing your suit, I burned a hole in the seat of your trousers.' 'Don't worry about it,' I said. 'You've forgotten that I have an extra pair of trousers for that suit.' 'Oh, I remembered alright,' she replied, 'I cut a piece from them to patch the hole.'

When Katie was in one of her disobedient moods her mother told her to behave herself. 'I will for a fiver,' replied Katie. 'You shouldn't ask for money to be good,' Mary said. 'You should be good for nothing – just like your father.'

Helen picked up the burger with both hands and crammed it into her mouth. 'Another bite like that, young lady,' I told her, 'and you'll have to leave the table.' 'Another bite like that,' she replied, 'and I'll be finished.'

One day I found Liz playing with her new housekeeping set. 'Are you washing dishes?' I asked. 'Yes,' she replied, 'and I'm drying them too, because I'm not married yet.' Hugh, you have been warned.

And a word of advice to you both: the best way to get the last word in any argument is to say 'sorry'.

If I were asked for a recipe for a long, happy marriage, I would say the formula lies in two simple words: 'Yes, dear'.

Advice to the bridegroom? Easy. When she hands you a dishcloth, blow your nose and hand it back.

Rodney and Cassandra first met in a revolving door and they've been going round together ever since.

As we were on our way to the wedding this morning, my wife turned to me and said, 'You know, you don't seem quite as well dressed as when we were married 25 years ago.' I replied, 'Well I don't know why not, I'm wearing the same suit.'

Ladies and Gentlemen, will you please stand, raise your glasses and drink a toast to the health and happiness of the bride and groom!

For the bridegroom

I would like to say a word of thanks to the bridesmaids. You did your job magnificently. Obviously I will use you every time I get married from now on.

Roger will be getting up to speak in a moment or two, and I can tell you he has some very unusual material, beginning with his suit.

I do not deserve the good things that have been said of me – but I will try to deserve them, and to be worthy of my wife.

I can't imagine a happier way to start married life than with our family and friends around us.

It takes two women to make a good husband – and the first one is his mother.

I asked her father if I could marry her and he said, 'Just leave your name and phone number and we'll be in contact if nothing better comes up.'

Next I must thank Faruq for being best man, though I'm not sure how thankful to be because I haven't heard his speech yet.

I think Donny's suit looks terrific. I know he won't mind if I let you all into a little secret – he always wears it when he goes to our monthly football social evenings [*or whatever*]. As we left for the church this morning, little Jimmy grabbed him by the arm and asked why he was wearing it today when he knew it always gives him such a headache the next morning.

Thank you for all your wonderful gifts. I can't tell you how much they mean to us – but I should have a better idea after the honeymoon, once I've spoken to the guy in the pawn shop.

I told Sue, 'Now we're married I want you to stick to your washing, ironing, cooking, cleaning and shopping . . . No wife of mine is going to work!'

They say marriage is a lottery. If it is, I have hit the jackpot.

Those of you who do not know Fred are the luckiest people in the world. That's because the pleasure of getting to know him lies ahead of you.

They say a girl grows to be like her mother; well, I can only hope it is true.

These delightful/charming [*safer than beautiful*] young ladies have done a great job in helping Sarah up the aisle – although I hope she came to the church of her own free will.

I have one final duty – no, not duty, pleasure – and that is to propose a toast to the health of the bridesmaids ... Ladies and Gentlemen, the bridesmaids!

For the best man

Ladies and Gentlemen, this is truly an historic day! [Followed by an anniversary hook.]

Ladies and Gentlemen, as Henry VIII said to each of his wives in turn, 'I shall not keep you long'! [Or some other humour hook.]

On behalf of the bridesmaids I would like to thank John for that toast. But to be honest I don't think he did them justice. Never mind – today who can blame him? Clearly he only has eyes for Janet. I'm still single and emotionally unblinkered and I think they are the most delightful set of bridesmaids I've ever seen.

My job today is to talk of Steven – and there are no skeletons in his cupboard – or so I thought ...

Doesn't Dean look great? They made wonderful suits in the 'eighties.

Greg told me he's going to buy you all a drink – and a straw each so you can share it.

If I ever needed a brain transplant, I'd choose Jim's because I'd want one that had never been used.

There is absolutely nothing wrong with Steve that a miracle can't fix.

Lee is a man of many parts – some still in working order.

Milek is very responsible. If there's a problem, you can be sure he's responsible.

I'm supposed to sing the bridegroom's praises and tell you all about his good points. Unfortunately, I can't sing, and I can't think of any good points.

Roy, if Audrey doesn't treat you as she should – be thankful.

It only takes one drink to get Steve drunk – the fourteenth.

He made that speech for nothing and, I'm sure you'll agree, he was worth every penny.

Jack became a millionaire last week. He didn't win the Lottery – he just took his empties back to the off-licence.

Paul told me he bought his suit for a ridiculous figure. Looking at him today, I'm afraid I must agree.

Ronnie is so unlucky, if he were to be reincarnated he'd probably come back as himself.

He was so ugly when he was born, they didn't know whether to buy a cot or a cage.

I think the world of him. Mind you, look at the state the world's in.

Geoff was never late for school – mainly because he never went.

The time has come for me, too, to take a wife. The only question remains: Whose wife to take?

My ambition is to be the last man on earth – so that I can find out if all those girls were telling the truth.

Pete's a man of rare gifts. He hasn't given one in years.

Every once in a while we have the opportunity to talk of a man of high achievement, transparent integrity and penetrating intellect. Not today though.

Debs finds Duggie very attractive. Then again, she is on heavy medication.

I have to say to you, that, in all the years I have known him, no one has ever questioned his intelligence. In fact, I've never heard anyone mention it.

Since we met nearly ten years ago, there hasn't been a day when I haven't thought about him. And I haven't thought about him today either.

Luke, I'm afraid you'll find that a wedding ring is like a tourniquet. It stops your circulation.

The trouble with being best man at a wedding is that you never get the chance to prove it.

They're such a busy couple: he's never found her in and she's never found him out.

Joe is a very modest man – and he has plenty to be modest about.

Noel is a man of hidden talents. I just hope some day he'll find them.

You may have noticed how few single people were invited to the wedding. I will let you into a secret: that was Ray's idea. He's very astute. He told me that if he invited only married people all the presents would be clear profit.

There's nothing I wouldn't do for Ryan, and I know there's nothing he wouldn't do for me. In fact, we spend our lives doing nothing for each other.

A man like Alan only comes along once in a lifetime – I'm only sorry it had to be during *my* lifetime.

I told my wife that we hadn't been able to agree on anything during our four years of marriage. 'Five years,' she replied.

I have already congratulated the groom. I said, 'Jason, you will always look back on this day as the happiest day of your life.' This was yesterday.

I want to refute this vicious rumour that's been going around here today that the bride and groom *had* to get married. That's a wicked lie. They could easily have waited another fortnight.

There's no doubt about it, men have better taste than women. After all, Paul chose Christina – but Christina chose Paul.

This marriage will last a lifetime. And, as you know, that's unusual these days. I know a couple who broke up before their wedding pictures were developed. And they used one of those paranoid cameras.

Gavin doesn't know the meaning of the word meanness. Mind you, he doesn't know the meaning of lots of other words either.

For the bride
My husband and I . . .

I'm very glad to break with tradition and say a few words of my own on this happy occasion.

My father knew that the most important thing he could do for his children was to love their mother.

And thank you for your wonderful wedding presents – with all those saucepans and toasters I only hope he likes boiled toast.

My mother told me that thirty years of marriage have taught her that the best way for a wife to have a few minutes to herself is to start doing the dishes.

Mum told me the only time a woman really succeeds in changing a man is when he's a baby – so I still have time to change Simon.

The longer I live, the more beautiful life becomes.

We've found a great way to settle our arguments; he admits he's wrong and I admit I'm right.

My granny told me that all girls should learn how to cook and clean the house. She said it would come in handy in case I couldn't find a husband.

He will make all the important decisions and I'll make all the insignificant ones – he'll decide when we should support America; whether we should scrap the House of Lords; and if we should change our voting system to PR . . . I'll decide when we should start a family; whether we should move house; and if he'll still be allowed out to watch United.

The other day I saw my husband facing a mirror with his eyes closed. I asked him what he was doing and he said he was trying to see what he looked like when he was asleep.

Meeting Andy was like opening your first bottle of champagne; marrying him is like drinking it.

He's no Einstein and I'm always on a diet. That's why we'll stay together through thick and thin.

This is my happiest day since I was in the arms of another woman's husband – my mother's.

And thanks to my own parents for taking care of me so well all my life and also for recognising that Alan was the right man to hand me over to. Alan Jones, this is your wife!

REHEARSING AD-LIBS

Rod Stewart sang about 'well rehearsed ad-lib lines'. A good speech-maker must be able to think on his or her feet but here are a few lines you could use under the right circumstances:

A speech-maker isn't around when required

I think Wayne must be up on the roof. I suppose it's my fault really, I shouldn't have told him the drinks were on the house. We'd better send out a search-party . . .

Your microphone starts playing up

Well, Mike, that is the end of our double act; I'm going solo. [*Then speak without it.*]

You forget a name or get it wrong

I'm so sorry, there are three things I always forget: names, faces and, er . . . I can't remember the other.

A glass or bottle smashes

I'm pleased you're having such a smashing time.

A tray falls

No, please, save your applause until I've finished.

A vehicle with a siren passes nearby

Well I'd better wind up before they come to get me.

Someone arrives late

Please come in. Sit down there. I'm so glad you could make it [*don't embarrass them by saying it sarcastically*]. You've arrived just in time to toast Babs and Jack. I was just telling everyone how they met while they were working for . . .

A waiter keeps rushing around in front of you

I think he must have a train to catch.

Someone interrupts (good-natured)

Yes, Bill, I do remember that – how could I forget it? And I also remember something that happened a few months later [*then back to your speech*].

Someone continually interrupts (bad-natured)

[*A tricky situation because he or she is someone's guest. Try to be amusing.*] I suggest you lean against the wall – that's plastered too.

The weather is atrocious or too good

I shall keep this short, in case we get snowed in/swept away in the storm/before all the ice melts.

A catch-all when anything at all goes wrong

Lisa, I hope that camcorder is still running. That is certain to be worth £250.

5

Using Your Voice Well

This chapter is about speaking skills and voice skills. If you are not used to speaking in public, you will find it useful first to assess your current speaking skills and make any improvements necessary to turn yourself into a *competent* public speaker. You may then wish to go on to consider the main features of a good public speaking voice and undertake a range of exercises that will enhance your voice and transform you into a *polished* public speaker.

Whichever programme or programmes you follow, remember that your voice is the main means of communicating with your audience and your aim must always be to speak fluently, intelligibly, animatedly and with confidence in order to convey genuine:

- ♦ joy and ease
- ♦ sincerity
- ♦ enthusiasm.

Your joy and ease will make your audience feel comfortable. Your sincerity will convince them you mean every word you say. And your enthusiasm will be infectious.

So how well *do* you speak? Do you speak loudly enough? Do you vary your pitch and tone? Do you pronounce each word correctly and distinctly? You probably don't know because you never listen to yourself. To be an effective communicator, you *must* listen to your own voice and practise different ways of getting your message across. For this reason you will need to get hold of a video camera or audio cassette player before you proceed.

If you decide to work on your speaking skills only, it is still well worth reading this entire chapter once because an awareness and understanding of voice features will be useful in itself, if it encourages a greater variety in speech.

ASSESSING YOUR CURRENT SKILLS

Every speaker needs those basic abilities which hold and retain an audience's attention. The key to avoiding tedium is variety: pace, style, pitch, tone. Try to inject a sparkle into your speech. Emphasise your main points. Convey the true meaning of your words. Express your deepest feelings.

This useful tip comes from actor David Suchet:

> Imagine that your audience is blind. They cannot see you. Because you will have to get into their ears, the energy in your voice will change and grow immediately. It will happen subconsciously. It will make you speak very differently.

The best way to find out how well you speak is to record yourself and then assess your performance against the guidelines which follow. Obviously it is sensible to choose a speech similar to the actual one you will be making on the big day. So take a look at the model speeches in Chapter 8. If you will be proposing a toast to the happy couple, you should choose model speech 1; if you are the bridegroom, choose model speech 22; and if you are the best man, choose model speech 41.

Read your speech through a number of times until you are familiar with it. Pretend this is your *actual* speech and then record yourself presenting it.

Now play the tape back and assess yourself against these guidelines:

- ◆ speed

- ◆ pausing

- ◆ articulation

- ◆ enunciation

- ◆ pronunciation

- ◆ modulation

- ◆ pitch

- ◆ repetition

- ◆ projection.

Don't worry about complicated words like 'articulation', 'enunciation' and 'modulation'. As we shall now see, the words may be difficult but the concepts are quite straightforward.

IMPROVING YOUR SPEAKING SKILLS

Speed

Time yourself presenting the speech. You will need to talk more slowly than you do normally. This allows your audience to absorb and consider what you are saying – and have plenty of time to laugh at your jokes!

Try to aim at about 100 words per minute (wpm). This is a little slower than you should speak, but the flow of adrenalin you will experience when you stand and deliver will speed you up to the right speed (about 130 wpm). If you rehearse at 130 words a minute you'll probably speed up to around 160 wpm which is too fast. At 100 wpm model speech 1 should have lasted about 4 minutes, speech 22 about 3½ minutes and speech 41 about 4½ minutes.

If you are within 30 seconds either way of your target time, that's fine. If you are not, you will need to adjust your pace. Remember that if you are speaking too quickly, you will need to say the words more slowly, not leave long gaps between each sentence.

Pausing

Have you punctuated your speech with short pauses, such as:

Reverend Green, Ladies and Gentlemen – [*pause*] Friends . . .

But let's face it, Karen is a very lucky lady too. [*pause*] No, I don't mean . . .

Talking of words, do you know what the name Kevin actually means? [*pause*] Well, believe it or not . . .

Pauses are the valleys that let listeners see the peaks. A pause can create anticipation in an audience, and heighten its attention for whatever follows. It can be used to good effect:

- before you start

- before an important phrase or sentence, or perhaps mid-sentence

- before a change in style, such as humour to seriousness

- before your close

- before your toast

- before you sit down.

Articulation

This means speaking distinctly. Listen to your tape again. Did you speak clearly? Did you say *Ladies and Gentlemen* or *Ladiesangentlemen*? If you need to improve your articulation, try:

- moving your lips more than you would normally

- emphasising the consonants slightly more

- leaving a very short pause between each word.

Enunciation

This means emphasising key words, syllables and phrases, for example:

the best way to get the last word in any argument is to say '*sorry*'.

happiest day *so far* that is . . .

well I don't know about *Bells*, but I work with Kevin at Fenn Street School and I can tell you he is one of the best *Teachers* I know.

We all do this in conversation, but it is a good idea to exaggerate slightly more when giving a speech. It adds variety, as well as bringing out important points. However, be careful where you place your emphasis. Consider any sentence, for example:

The man said the woman was a fool.

and the effect of putting emphasis on different words.

The man, said the woman, *was a fool.*

The man said *the woman was a fool.*

Changing the emphasis can alter the meaning, so check that you always put the emphasis on the right word(s).

Pronunciation

Were you able to pronounce every word?

Poor pronunciation makes a bad impression and may confuse your audience. If in doubt, leave it out. There are plenty of other suitable words you can substitute that you *can* pronounce.

Modulation

How much did you vary your pitch and tone?

Modulation is essential to keep your audience's interest and to guide them through your points. Most of us modulate in conversation, but some people sink into monotone when making a speech. If your speech sounded a bit flat, listen to TV presenters or announcers on the radio. Notice how they use modulation to introduce a new topic, break up points, convey whether comments are serious or light-hearted, and so on. Then try presenting the speech again, varying your pitch and tone.

Pitch

Nervousness raises the pitch of the voice. So, when starting your speech, your voice is likely to be higher than normal. You should deliberately lower your voice a little to compensate. If you *think* about your words as you speak, your pitch will vary automatically.

Repetition

While this is to be avoided in written work, it can be used to great effect in a speech. When repeating words or phrases, it is best to vary the tone and pitch, for example:

We will have a wonderful life – a *wonderful* life together.

Projection

The last – and most important – question is: Will everyone be able to hear you? If not, all else is lost. If you need to improve your projection, stand up straight, and take two or three deep breaths. Then start speaking, concentrating on throwing your voice (but not shouting). Practise until you can project your voice with ease. When making your speech, check whether everyone can hear you by watching the faces of people furthest from you. If they seem to be straining to hear you, then you will need to speak up.

Here are some hints that will help you project your voice more effectively:

♦   Keep your head up.

♦   Open your mouth more than during normal speech.

♦   Use clear consonants.

♦   Speak more slowly than usual.

Once you have drafted your script, record it and assess your presentation against these same nine guidelines. A speech is like a pair of shoes – it will always benefit from a little more polishing.

DEVELOPING YOUR VOICE SKILLS

Voice skills are those more advanced abilities required by speakers who want to develop a truly effective speaking voice. This section will provide an insight into the features of a good voice and will suggest a range of techniques and exercises to limber up your vocal apparatus. We all have the potential for a stronger, richer, more interesting voice; one that conveys that magical mixture of confidence, vitality and ease.

Features of a good voice

What, technically, makes for a good voice? A good voice is the result of the following features:

- **Breathing** support for the voice is adequate for fluent, clear expression.

- **Jaw and throat** are open so that there is no hard edge or blocked tone to the voice.

- **Articulation** of speech sounds is clear and precise, any national or regional accent being irrelevant.

- **Pitch** is suitable for the speaker, given their age and gender, and a variety in intonation is included to give life and energy to the tone of the voice.

- **Resonance** is balanced: the tone of the voice is not nasal, chesty, plummy or thin.

- **Projection and volume** are adequate for the size of room and audience, without being monotonously loud or forced.

- **Speed and rhythm** are appropriate for the material, and pauses are used meaningfully.

FOLLOWING THE 28-DAY VOICE DEVELOPMENT PROGRAMME

You will be amazed how your voice can be transformed in just one month. Practising the following exercises at least five times a week during the run-up to the wedding will make your voice stronger and more open and flexible. But any section can be done on its own, once you decide what could be improved in your voice. If even that's too much for you, at least sing in the bath or join in a few Saturday afternoon soccer chants. When it comes to the voice, it is a case of use it or lose it.

Breathing

Most of us breathe with only the top part of our body which means we are not fully lowering the diaphragm or expanding the lungs. This kind of restricted breathing stifles emotional expression and can result in tension in the neck, throat and voice.

To find out whether you are breathing correctly, try these two simple exercises:

♦ Put one hand on the upper part of your chest and the other on the top of the abdomen (the top of the bulge below your chest). Establish a regular pattern of slow, deep breathing. As you inhale, which hand rises first? It should be your *lower* hand. If it is not, you re not making use of the lungs' full capacity.

♦ Place your hands across your stomach with just the tips of your fingers touching. Bell out the stomach as you inhale. As you exhale, press your fingers down onto the now flattened stomach. As it bells out again, are your fingers being separated and drawn apart, and do they come together again as you breathe out? They *should* do.

If you are not breathing correctly, perform this exercise regularly until you have learned to breathe deeply, using your abdomen as well as your chest:

♦ Rest your hands on your rib cage at the sides, just above the waist. Breathe out completely. Inhale gently through the nose, allowing your abdomen to swell. Breathe in more air, this time allowing your ribs and then your chest to expand but making sure that your shoulders do not raise during the process. Hold your breath for a couple more seconds before exhaling all the air slowly through the mouth. Notice how your rib cage shrinks beneath your hands as your abdomen is pulled in. Repeat 10 times.

Any physical exercise which has an aerobic benefit will also help you breathe correctly. It takes time for the body to change its ingrained breathing habits. But it's well worth persevering, as lower chest deep breathing is much better for voice and general health.

Jaw and throat exercises

Let your jaw drop comfortably and as wide as you can. Imagine how many fingers you could place horizontally between your teeth. Most people think three or four. Try it. There's probably room for just one or two. We think we open our mouths – and thereby free our jaws – far more than we really do. And as voice trainer Christina Schule puts it: 'You can't sing Wall's Cornetto, or speak in a mock Italian accent, or speak well with a tight jaw.'

♦ Stand up and stretch. Yawn loudly and feel the deep hollow sound as your throat opens. Yawn again, this time pushing your tongue out and feeling the stretch. Breathe in while your tongue is still out, feeling the cool air in the space at the back of your mouth.

♦ Chew an imaginary piece of chewing-gum with big open-mouthed movements. Feel the stretching of your cheeks, jaw and mouth. Repeat the months of the year as you chew: *January*, *February*, *March* . . .

♦ Hum — *mmmmmmmm* — on to gently closed lips. Feel a tickly, tingling sensation in your lips. This means the sound is 'placed' forward in the mouth, rather than tightly pushed in the throat, or held at the back of the mouth. Repeat 5 times. Then open your mouth, with the hum still going, into a wide, clear *mmmmmmmm aaaaaaaah.* Feel the sound streaming out. Sing *mmmmmmmm aaaaaaaah 1-2-3-4-5.* Now, with the same 'forward' sensation, speak on one breath the days of the week: *Monday*, *Tuesday*, *Wednesday* . . .

Learning to articulate

Articulation is the production of different sounds. There are more than 50 different sounds in English and when you produce any of them you are articulating. Repeat each of these exercises 10 times:

♦ Open your mouth very wide and then close it.

- Round your lips and protrude them as far as you can and practise the sound *oooooooo*.

- Spread your lips back in a big smile. Feel the muscles pulling around your chin and neck area. Practise the sound *eeee*. Then make the sound *eeoo*.

- Thrust your upper lip forward; thrust your lower lip forward.

- Stretch your upper lip down; stretch your lower lip up.

- Raise the right side of your mouth; raise the left side of your mouth. Be sure the whole of your face is involved in the movement. It is necessary to have the muscles in your face moving freely for expression.

- Protrude your tongue without touching your upper or lower lip. This will be helpful for production of sounds like *th*.

- Point the tip of your tongue up and touch your top lip, then the right corner of your mouth, then the left, then point it down towards your chin.

- Rotate your tongue around your mouth over your upper teeth, then your lower teeth.

- Raise the tip of your tongue and touch the gum ridge behind your upper teeth, slowly bringing it back towards your palate.

- Let the tip of your tongue touch the roof of your mouth. Flap it up and produce a strong *lah lah lah nah nah nah*.

- Open your mouth as wide as you can and say: *a e i o u.*

- Say: *I want to go to Ward 10* (not 'I wanna go t' Ward N') and: *Give me the hat* (not 'Gimme the 'at).

- Now say: *childhood, witchcraft, brightness* (not 'chilhood, witcraft, brighness).

- Practise saying these tongue twisters:

    The sixth sheik's sixth sheep's sick.

    She sells sea-shells on the sea-shore.

    The Leith police dismisseth us.

Pitch

Pitch is the musical note of the voice.

- Yawn, sliding your voiced yawn down from the highest to the lowest note you can make. Yawn again, this time sliding your voiced yawn from your lowest to highest note. Repeat 5 times.

- Speak the sentence:

    I don't think we should go this week.

    on 5 different pitches:

    high
    medium high
    middle
    medium low
    low

Listen to their different effects on the sound of the sentence.

♦ Choose one of the model speeches in Chapter 8 (a different one each time you do this exercise). Tape record yourself presenting it, letting your voice go up and down in pitch when it feels appropriate. Play it back. Does it sound lively and energetic? Or too much like a child's bedtime story? Or the latest news report from Moscow? Record other versions until you are satisfied with your rendition.

Resonance

Hum out a loud *mmmmmmmmm*, imagining the sound going up into your nose and forehead. Say, *meemeemeemeemee*. Say, *This nasal twang sounds horrible*. Now hum again. This time, imagine the sound is echoing in your chest. Beat your upper and lower chest with your hand as you hum, feeling the vibrations. Say, *maamaamaamaamaa*. Say, *I can feel the booming chest quality of my voice*. Now hum so you feel the tingle on your lips. Open the sound into *mmm aaaaw*. Hear the loud, open quality. Imagine a balance of head and chest tone; a balance that feels just right for your voice.

Speak about today's weather with that same balanced voice and clear forward sound.

Projection and volume

Being able to project your voice comes with mastery of correct breathing and self-confidence.

♦ Take a deep breath into the diaphragm and try 'sending' your voice to a different place: the other side of the room, the next room, the next floor. Speak this sentence:

I am delighted to be here today.

Say it 5 times. Imagine the sound streaming to:

1 person
10 people
50 people
100 people
500 people.

♦ Choose another model speech and perform it to an imaginary audience of approximately the same size as will be at the wedding reception. Speak one sentence loud, one soft, and so on. Experiment with volume.

Speed and rhythm

Speaking with a 'machine-gun' delivery, placing equal emphasis on each word and without pause, sounds very monotonous.

Read these two sentences:

Becky lives in Bath.
Rebecca resides in Somerset.

Same girl; same place; different descriptions. How long did it take to recite each sentence'. More-or-less the same, with the second taking just a little longer? The first sentence has four syllables, whilst the second has nine, yet you probably spoke each word in the second sentence much more quickly than the words in the first, with emphasis on certain syllables only: Reb*ecca resides in Som*erset. This highlights the danger of reading scripts. It is all too easy to machine-gun your delivery and lose the natural rise and fall of your voice.

Say the following out loud, first without and then with pauses:

> [*pause*] Today we look back at the single lives of Mark and Cleo, [*pause*] and also look forward into the crystal ball to see what lies ahead for Mr and Mrs Antony, [*pause*] Well you don't need to be a Mystic Meg to know their future, [*pause*] It's going to be more, [*pause*] much more of the same.

I'm sure you will agree that the second version was much better. Did you notice how pausing also caused you to vary your speed and rhythm? How long did it take you to say it? At l00wpm it should have been about 30 seconds.

A FINAL WORD . . .

Concentrate on your voice development during the run-up to the wedding, but then forget all about it on the big day. Your voice will have improved dramatically over the last month, and it is now time to simply relax and be yourself. As actors are taught, you must:

> 'Dig deep to fly high and then throw it all away.'

6

Giving Out the Right Non-verbal Messages

COMMUNICATING WITH YOUR WHOLE BODY

When considering wedding speeches, many people concentrate solely on the spoken word. They forget that their unspoken physical messages – their body language – will also have a major impact. An audience does a lot more than just listen to a speech – it *experiences* it. Everything about a speaker's manner and demeanour contributes to the overall impression and feeling an audience takes away. Body language is potent. We speak with our vocal cords, but we communicate with our whole body.

All the main elements of body language – stance and posture, movement and gestures, and eye contact and facial expression – are immediately related and interdependent. You must send out an overall co-ordinated non-verbal message. And this message must also be consistent with your verbal message or you will lose all credibility. In the words of the old Chinese proverb: Watch out for the man whose stomach does not move when he laughs.

It is not possible to successfully fake body language, but it is possible to learn how to project yourself far more positively, thereby showing your audience that you are:

♦ sincere

♦ enthusiastic

♦ natural

♦ friendly

♦ and proficient.

What hidden messages do you give out when you speak? If you are unsure, video yourself as you rehearse, or watch yourself in a mirror, or ask a kind but critical friend. You will probably find that you need to work on one or more of the following:

♦ stance and posture

♦ movement and gestures

♦ eye contact and facial expression.

However, remember that while each of these may be considered in isolation, a change made to any one of them will also have a direct and immediate effect on the others.

CONVEYING CONFIDENCE AND INTEGRITY

Your stance and posture are important. You are making a fundamental statement with your body. An aligned, upright posture conveys a message of confidence and integrity.

Early man frightened his enemies by inflating his chest and spreading his arms to present a much wider profile (see Figure 2). Modern man uses exactly the same technique, consciously or unconsciously, when he wants to convince others of his dominance (see Figure 3).

Standing correctly

Stand upright with your feet shoulder-width apart and very slightly turned out. You can then shift your weight from one side to the other, if you have to, without being noticed. Keep well clear of the table; leaning on it would make you look aggressive, and you could end up crying over spilt champagne. Don't put your hands in your pockets or grasp them together unnaturally at your back or front. Either hold your cue card in one hand or place it on the table in front of you. This allows you to glance at it from time to time while still giving you the freedom to use your hands to help express yourself.

Don't shield yourself

Our instincts tell us that anyone who shields himself – even with just his arms – is being defensive; while anyone who does not shield himself is perceived as friendly (see Figures 4 and 5).

REINFORCING YOUR VERBAL MESSAGES

You should be far more than just a talking head. You don't want to be so motionless that you look like a statue on loan from Madame Tussaud's. But, equally, you shouldn't attempt an impersonation of John McCririck's Saturday afternoon arm-waving histrionics. It is perfectly possible to make simple hand gestures which reinforce your verbal messages without

Fig. 2. The caveman's aggressive body language.

This domineering stance is
unsuitable for making a
wedding speech

A friendly, upright, open,
unthreatening stance is far
preferable

Fig. 3. Don't threaten the guests!

Fig. 4. Early man used a shield to defend himself.

Closed arms are seen as defensive and negative

Open arms and open palms are considered friendly and positive

Fig. 5. Don't defend yourself against the guests!

distracting your audience. Avoid any movement or gesture that is likely to be seen as negative or inappropriate.

Avoiding hostile gestures

Early man attacked his victims by holding a weapon above their heads and bringing it down with great force (see Figure 6). Our legacy from this is that, even today, our ancestral memories perceive similar positions and movements as hostile (see Figure 7).

Practising your gestures

When you begin your speech you may feel more at ease if you keep your elbows at your sides with your hands held lightly in front of you. Once you get underway you will relax and your hand gestures will come naturally. As you gesture, your shoulders and head will adopt the appropriate position automatically. All your gestures should be clear, consistent and definitive. Most of all, they should be spontaneous – from within you – otherwise you will come over as robotic and insincere.

Here are a few sentences often heard during wedding speeches. Speak them out loud and support your words with appropriate and expressive gestures. If possible, video yourself. Failing that, watch yourself in a mirror or ask friends how effective your gestures are.

♦   'It was a beautiful wedding.'

♦   'I'm going to let you into a little secret about our groom . . .'

♦   'Doesn't she look elegant?'

Fig. 6. The hostile caveman.

Hands and fingers pointing
upwards and finger-wagging
sweeping movements are
seen as threatening

Open palms with fingers
downward are seen as
unthreatening and friendly

Fig. 7. Don't be hostile to the guests!

- 'This is the happiest day of my life!'

- 'Please raise your glasses and join me in a toast to . . .'

Being sincere

Movement and gesture give additional meaning to your words and add variety to your performance. However, there must always be good reasons for them or they will become no more than distractions. Worse still, if they are not consistent with your verbal message and the rest of your body language you will come over as insincere.

Identifying your bad habits

We all have at least one bad habit or gesture. Use video, mirror or friend to identify yours. Do any of the faults listed below apply to you?

- playing with your watch

- talking with your hand in front of your mouth

- pushing your glasses back up your nose

- jingling coins in your pocket

- waving your hands about for no reason

- rustling your notes

- shuffling your feet

- swaying

- making pointless gestures.

Try to eliminate any such habits because they are a powerful means of distraction. Your audience will become preoccupied with when they will happen next and will start watching you rather than listening to you.

USING YOUR HEAD

Eye contact and facial expression are crucial aspects of effective communication because they gain and then maintain an audience's attention, create rapport, and give you valuable feedback as to how well you are coming over. The worst thing you can do, apart from mumbling inaudibly, is not to look at your audience. You should have memorised your opening and closing lines, so *look* at your audience as you deliver them. During the middle section of your speech try to keep your head up from your cue card for at least 90 per cent of the time.

Maintaining eye contact

Entertainers use the so-called lighthouse technique to maintain eye contact with their audiences. This means beaming all around the room slowly, tracing an imaginary X or Z shape but continually varying the size and shape of the letter to avoid your eye sweeps becoming routine and predictable. Look at everyone and make this deliberate and noticeable. Stop occasionally to look at individuals for just long enough to give the impression that you are talking to them without picking them out for special attention – unless, of course, you *are* picking them out for special attention. Even then keep the entire audience involved as illustrated below.

[*Eye contact with the audience generally*]
I would like to tell you something about my father that might surprise you.

[*Pause and turn to your father*]
Dad, if it wasn't for you I wouldn't be standing here today.
[*Pause and turn back to the audience generally*]
This man helped me at a time when nobody else . . . (tell your story)
[*Pause and turn back to your father*]
Thank you, dad.
[*Pause and turn back to the audience generally and continue your speech*]

Conveying emotion

But you must do more than simply look at your audience; you must use your eyes and your facial expression to convey emotion. This isn't as difficult as it may sound. You do it every day. Practise using your eyes and facial expressions to convey: happiness, surprise, optimism, mirth, joy, love, confidence, sincerity.

Can you match up the captions and characters in Figure 9?

Smiling

There is nothing more captivating than a smile. It shows warmth and friendliness and says: I'm really pleased to be here giving this speech. It's going to be great fun and we're all going to have a wonderful time! So smile, smile – and then smile (see Figure 8).

Fig. 8. Smile, smile and smile again.

Captivating your audience

The effectiveness of your speech will depend, to a large extent, on how you look and sound. Relaxed stance and upright posture, purposeful economy of movement and fluid gestures, lively eyes and facial expression, and expressive voice, will all capture your audience's attention and greatly enhance the power of your message.

Fig. 9. Facial expressions.

7

Having Self-Confidence and Coping with Nerves

The script is written and the presentation rehearsed. The hard work is behind you. What you must do now is relax and get yourself into the right state of mind. This means thinking positively, visualising success and dealing with any possible attack of nerves.

THINKING POSITIVELY

Tell yourself that you are going to make a great speech. And *believe* it. The largely untapped power of positive thinking really is immense. Unfortunately, many speakers think they are going to fail, and this becomes a self-fulfilling prophecy. As Henry Ford put it: 'Whether you think you will succeed or whether you think you will fail, you will probably be right.'

Some people may find this anonymous poem inspirational. Needless to say, it applies equally to women:

IF

If you think you are beaten, you are;
If you think you dare not, you don't;
If you'd like to win, but think you can't,
It's almost certain you won't;
If you think you'll lose you've lost.
For out of the world we find
Success begins with a fellow's will –
It's all in the state of mind.
If you think you're outclassed, you are.
You've got to think high to rise;
You've got to be sure of yourself before
You can ever win a prize.
Life's battles don't always go
To the stronger or faster man,
But sooner or later the man who wins
Is the one who *thinks* he can.

VISUALISING SUCCESS

Visualisation is the planting of mental images into the subconscious mind. These images must be vivid and real – you must be able to *see*, to *hear*, to *smell*, to *touch*, to *taste* and to truly *live them*. It is a way to free yourself from previously accepted boundaries and barriers. We are all victims of programming. As a child, you may have been told, 'your spelling is atrocious'. Your subconscious mind would have accepted this (even if it were not true) and it would have made sure that from that moment you really *were* a poor speller. Through visualisation you can re-programme your subconscious mind to accept that you can spell well. In exactly the same way, you can pre-programme your subconscious mind to accept you are not nervous and you are going to make an excellent speech.

If you can vividly *imagine* an event happening, it will greatly strengthen the likelihood of it *actually* happening. This is not a crankish idea. Controlled medical experiments have proved it to be true. When a patient visualises cancer cells being engulfed by anti-bodies in the bloodstream, it is far more likely to happen than if that patient just lies back and lets nature take its course.

You are now going to watch a film clip with a difference – because the screenwriter, the director and the star will be *you*. Close your eyes and visualise yourself rising to speak. You are looking good. Feel the warmth of the audience. You are surrounded by family and friends. You pause for a moment and then begin. They love your opening hook. But it gets better; your stories and little jokes wow them. Laughter one minute, tears the next. They are eating out of your hand. Then comes that emotion-packed big finish. Nobody could have topped that. Listen to their cheers and applause. Now that's what I call a wedding speech!

The best times to present your subconscious mind with such a positive visualisation is when you are mentally calm and physically relaxed, when you are in the hypnogogic state that precedes sleep, or when you are in a state of light sleep.

MAKING FEAR YOUR FRIEND

But even the best-prepared and most psyched-up speaker can suffer from a sudden attack of the collywobbles. It is perfectly natural and normal to feel a little nervous when delivering a speech. In fact, it helps if you do. The adrenalin will flow and you will be charged up and ready to give a really great performance.

However, if you feel too nervous the quality of your speech will suffer. So here are a few tricks of the trade to help you cope with your nerves (or at least conceal them), both before and during your speech.

As you sit there remind yourself that your audience will be on your side. This is a happy day. They are not a jury. They are willing you to do well. And, quite frankly, they won't give a damn if you do fluff a line or two.

Even if you are still feeling nervous, remember that you will be the only person in the room who knows it – 90 per cent of our nervousness is internal; only 10 per cent displays itself to the outside world. Unless you tell them you are nervous they won't know. So never, *never* tell them.

Whatever you do, don't drink too much. Booze is like success; it is great until it goes to your head. Bob Monkhouse's maxim was: never accept a drink before you speak; never refuse one after. Don't drink and drivel.

If you feel the pressure beginning to get to you, try one or two of these emergency relaxation techniques. They can be used anywhere and any time without anyone, except you, knowing it.

USING EMERGENCY RELAXATION TECHNIQUES

Breathing to reduce tension

1. Sit comfortably with your arms at your sides and breathe in deeply through your nose.

2. Hunch up your shoulders as high as you can, clench your fists, push your toes hard into the floor, tense your body even harder than it is now – and then still harder.

3. Hold your breath for a few seconds.

4. As you exhale slowly through your nose, loosen your shoulders and let them drop, unclench your fists and let your heels return to the floor. Imagine that your shoulders are dropping down as far as your waist and that your feet are so light that they are sinking into the ground.

Sitting at a table

1. Pull in your stomach muscles tightly. Relax.

2. Clench your fists tightly. Relax.

3. Extend your fingers. Relax.

4. Grasp the seat of your chair. Relax.

5. Press your elbows tightly into the side of your body. Relax.

6. Push your feet into the floor. Relax.

Spot relaxation

1. Imagine that your shoulders are very heavy.

2. Hunch them up.

3. Drop them down very slowly.

4. Gently tip your head forward and feel the muscles pulling up through the middle of your shoulder blades.

5. Move your head gently backwards and feel the tension in the muscles down the front of your neck.

6. Bring your head back to an upright position and breathe very deeply for a few moments.

Stopping negative thoughts

1. Tell yourself: *Stop!*

2. Breathe in and hold your breath.

3. Exhale slowly, relaxing your shoulders and hands.

4. Pause. Breathe in slowly, relaxing your forehead and jaw.

5. Remain quiet and still for a few moments.

Head in the clouds

1. Stare at the ceiling and visualise floating clouds.

2. Imagine you are drifting towards them.

3. Release your tension and watch it float away with the clouds.

4. Gradually return from the clouds, feeling calm, cool and collected in your thoughts.

Draining tension away

Imagine you are transparent and filled with your favourite colour liquid. The temperature is perfect. Then drain the liquid from your body through your fingers and toes. Feel the tension draining away with the fluid.

The decanter

Sit comfortably and imagine that your body is a decanter. The bottom of the bottle is your pelvis and hips and the top is your head. As you breathe in, picture the air as pure energy gradually filling up the decanter. Hold the energy for a few seconds and then see it slowly pouring out as you exhale.

The hammock

Imagine you have been walking along a beach for hours. You are very tired. Suddenly you spot a hammock at the top of a steep sand dune. You begin to climb the dune, but you are now becoming exhausted. *Only ten more steps to go, now nine* ... you can hardly stand up ... *now eight, seven, six* ... feel the agony of each step upwards ... *four, three* ... not far now ... *two, one*, you make it! Collapse into the hammock and relax completely.

The stairway

As you sit in your chair, pick a spot on the wall, slightly above your eye level, and stare at it. Do not allow your attention to waver. Take three long breaths, with normal breathing for about ten seconds between each of them. Each time you exhale think the word *relax*, and let every muscle and nerve in your body go loose and limp. After you have said *relax* for the third time, close your eyes. Imagine you are at the top of a stairway. At the bottom of the stairs is complete relaxation. Visualise yourself descending. With each step you will become more and more relaxed. *20*, deeper in relaxation; *19* deeper; *18* deeper; and so on down to *1*. At that point you will be completely relaxed.

Meditation of the bubble

Picture yourself sitting quietly and comfortably at the bottom of a clear lake. Every time you have a negative thought, imagine it inside a bubble which gently rises out of your vision towards the surface. Then calmly wait for your next thought. If it is negative, watch it slowly rise towards the surface in another bubble. If you prefer, visualise yourself sitting next to a campfire with all your negative words and images rising in puffs of smoke, or sitting on the bank of a river with all your tension, fears and anxieties inside logs which are gently floating away from you.

Your favourite place

Visualise your favourite place – real or imagined: past, present or future. This is your very own secret place; and because it is in your mind, no one else need ever know about it. Perhaps it is in a beautiful valley by a gently flowing stream; or perhaps it is in a spaceship travelling to Mars. It is entirely up to you. Use all your senses – *see* the blue sky, *hear* the gurgling stream, *smell* the scented flowers, *taste* the cool water, *touch* the warm grass. Really *be there*. This idea may sound silly, but it isn't, for one simple reason – it works. Remain at your favourite place until you feel perfectly relaxed and ready to return to face the real world.

COPING DURING YOUR SPEECH

However nervous most people feel before making a speech, their nerves will almost certainly evaporate once they are introduced and they begin to speak. Think about it this way: most footballers feel nervous, especially before a big game. But once they hear the shrill of the first whistle, their nerves seem to disappear. The reason? At that moment all their pent up tension is released and they can finally get on with the job in hand.

But if you do still feel nervous, here are a few tips to help you cope:

♦ As you begin your speech, smile naturally, find a few friendly faces and maintain plenty of eye contact with them. As your confidence grows, look more and more at other people around the rest of the room.

♦ Never admit that you are the slightest bit nervous.

♦ If you begin to shake, concentrate on your knees. Try to shift the shaking down to your kneecaps. You will find that most of it will evaporate en route. Whatever does arrive there will be hidden behind the table.

♦ Keep your notes on the table so they can't rattle or end up all over the floor.

♦ Don't draw attention to your hands.

♦ Don't hold a hand-mike; leave it on its stand.

♦ Be aware of any possibly annoying personal habit you may have – such as twitching – and make a positive effort to control it.

♦ If your mouth becomes dry and your throat tightens up, the obvious thing to do is to take a sip of water. But if this isn't possible, imagine you are sucking an orange.

But the best way to keep your nerves in check is to know that you have prepared a really great little speech. And make sure it *is* a little speech. As the mother whale said to her young: 'Remember, my dears, you can be harpooned only when you're spouting.' So don't go spouting on and on. Stand up to be seen, speak up to be heard, and then shut up to be appreciated. Good luck!

8

Fifty Model Speeches

Finally, it's time to put it all together by taking a look at some model speeches.

You can use these in one of three ways. You could select the one that best suits you and then adapt and personalise it, or take what you think to be the best bits from two or more speeches and adapt and personalise them, or plan your own speech from scratch after reading these just for inspiration.

The usual order of speeches is:

1. Proposal of a toast to the bride and groom (model speeches 1–21).
2. Response to the toast and proposal of a second toast (model speeches 22–40).
3. Response on behalf of the bridesmaids (model speeches 41–50).

Traditionally, the first speech is made by the bride's father or guardian; the second by the bridegroom; and the third by the best man or best girl. However, this pattern assumes that the bride has been brought up by two parents and today over two million people in Britain haven't been. So now it is perfectly acceptable for speeches to be made by other people – perhaps by a close relative or family friend, by the bride's mother, or by the bride herself. It all depends on the particular circumstances of the bride and groom.

MAKING YOUR CHOICE

For those of you who do not want to wade through all these model speeches, here is a summary of which of them best suit these particular personal circumstances.

One of the couple was brought up in a single-parent family: Model speeches 5, 6, 7, 18, 19, 20, 25, 26, 36 and 37.

One of their parents is recently deceased: Model speeches 3, 4, 16, 17, 23, 24, 34 and 35.

They already have a child: Model speeches 11, 12, 13, 30, 31 and 32.

There were no bridesmaids at the wedding: Model speeches 21, 39, 40, 47 and 48.

It is a second marriage: Model speeches 8, 9, 10, 27, 28 and 29.

Nobody should ever be forced to speak, if they do not want to. This is supposed to be a happy day, so no one should be forced to do anything. However, if anyone is going to speak, they should know about it well in advance, and they must know the precise *purpose* of their speech. Is it to propose a toast, to respond to a toast, or to do both?

The speeches should begin after the guests have finished eating. Make sure their glasses are charged *before* anyone speaks. If there is a toastmaster, he will say something like: 'Ladies and Gentlemen, pray silence for Mr Ben Nevis who will propose a toast to Mr Sydney and Mrs Pearl Harbour.' If there is no toastmaster, the best man should do the honours, possibly in a less formal manner: 'Ladies and Gentlemen, please be silent as Mr Ben Nevis proposes a toast to Mr Sydney and Mrs Pearl Harbour.'

Right, now let's take a look at 50 model speeches which, when adapted, personalised and possibly combined, should suit any particular set of circumstances.

PROPOSING A TOAST TO THE BRIDE AND GROOM

At a formal wedding reception this opening speech should include some positive comments about the couple and some optimistic thoughts about love and marriage. At a more informal wedding party, the speech can be more general. At either setting it must all build up to the toast.

A good speech includes the right balance of humour and seriousness, all applied with liberal helpings of sentiment. But what is the right balance? That depends on the personalities of the couple and their backgrounds and circumstances. For example, a very humorous speech would be out of place if one of their parents died last month. It also depends on *your* personality. Do you feel comfortable telling a joke? If you don't, don't do it.

Model speech 1: Bride's father

Formal reception

Reverend Green, Ladies and Gentlemen – Friends, 'We cannot fully enjoy life unless someone we love enjoys it with us.' Not my words, I'm afraid, although how I agree with them.

I cannot begin to tell you how delighted I am to see my daughter, Karen, looking so radiant as she begins a new chapter of her life – as the wife and partner of Richard. I know I'm also speaking for Mary when I say we are not losing Karen; we are merely entrusting her into Richard's care. And as we have got to know Richard well over the last few months, we have come to the inescapable conclusion that this will be very, very good care. He has shown himself to be exactly the sort of person we had always hoped Karen would marry: a man who knows where he's going in life – and how he's going to get there.

It seems like only yesterday that I found Karen playing with her new housekeeping set. 'Are you washing dishes?' I asked. 'Yes,' she replied, 'and I'm drying them as well because I'm not married yet.' Richard, you have been warned.

Looking around me, I see a picture of sartorial elegance. You'd put the Royal Ascot crowd to shame. But my wife isn't quite so sure about my appearance. As we were on our way to the wedding this morning, Mary turned to me and said, 'You know, you don't seem quite as well dressed as when we were married 25 years ago.' 'Well I don't know why not,' I replied, 'because I'm wearing the same suit.'

It is customary on an occasion such as this for the father of the bride to pass on a few words of wisdom about the institution of marriage. Well, if 25 years of blissful marriage have taught me anything – and I pass this advice on to both of you – it is that the best way to get the last word in any argument is to say 'sorry'. But better still, of course, why argue in the first place?

Everyone who knows Karen and Richard believe that this has been one of those marriages made in heaven, and I know you will all want to join me in wishing them a long and happy married life together. So please stand up, raise your glasses and drink to the health and happiness of Karen and Richard.

To Karen and Richard!

Model speech 2: Close family friend, relative or godfather

Formal reception – where the bride's father is present but does not make a speech.

Ladies and Gentlemen, Anne's father, Phil, and her mother, Liz, have done me the great honour of offering me the opportunity of making this little speech on this joyous occasion, and to propose a toast to the happy couple. When I asked why they chose me, Phil explained that it was because we've been friends for more years than he cares to remember and that I have known Anne for all her life. Not so, Phil, I missed the first 24 hours.

You know, this is truly a historic day! This day, the 13th of July, will always be remembered because of three world-famous events. Film actor Harrison Ford was born in 1942; Live Aid pop concerts raised millions for charity in 1985; and on this day in 200X, Tim married Anne!

It seems like only yesterday that Anne's weekends were taken up with tap dancing, ballet and the pony club. She called her pony Radish and used to go round telling everyone it was her horse Radish.

But seriously, we're all very proud of the wonderful work she does for sick animals. And it was while she was helping out down at the RSPCA that she first met Tim.

Over the last few months I've got to know Tim well and I've come to the conclusion that he's a very pleasant, hard-working man with immaculate tastes. After all, he supports United and he chose Anne, didn't he?

Friends, I am sure that this young couple will have a wonderful marriage and I would ask you to join me now in wishing them a long, happy and prosperous future together. Please stand and raise your glasses. I propose a toast to the health and happiness of Anne and Tim.

To Anne and Tim!

Model speech 3: Close family friend, relative or godfather
Formal reception – where the bride's father is recently deceased.

Ladies and Gentlemen, it is a great honour for me to be here with you all today on this joyous occasion. I have known Clare and her parents for many years. It was 1990 when

Henry, Sarah and a very young Clare became my next-door neighbours. Henry was an excellent gardener and he soon transformed not only his garden – but mine as well.

In fact we were in my greenhouse when he told me that Clare had met Francis. He spoke very highly of the young man on that June evening and on many subsequent occasions. Although we all greatly miss Henry, we can rejoice in the fact that he would have been absolutely delighted that Francis and Clare have become man and wife. And because his hopes and wishes have now been realised I feel that in a sense he is celebrating here with us today.

As you know, the wedding was postponed, but Clare is a girl well worth waiting for. Doesn't she look radiant? Henry would have been proud of her – as I'm sure Francis is. I have got to know Francis very well since we first met last summer and I know Clare has made a very wise choice. He's a hard-working lad who knows money comes first and last. You've got to make it first and then make it last. These young people have a very bright future ahead of them and I would like you all to join me in wishing them every success as they begin their married life together. So please raise your glasses and drink to the health and happiness of Clare and Francis.

To Clare and Francis!

Model speech 4: Bride's father

Formal reception – where one of the bridegroom's parents is recently deceased.

Ladies and Gentlemen, it's been quite a week. England hammered Holland, I won a few quid on the National and now, to crown it all, Ted married Carol. You know, I read in a newspaper the other day that marriage is going out of fashion. Well, you can't believe everything you read in newspapers. And even if it's true, have you ever seen two people so delighted to be out of fashion?

It seems only like yesterday that Carol's music was blasting through our household. I asked if I could borrow her CD for the evening. 'Do you fancy some heavy metal?' she asked. 'No, just a bit of peace and quiet,' I replied. Come to think about it, it *was* yesterday.

But 'if music be the food of love, play on' because that's how Carol got to meet Ted. At a gig – I think that's what you call it – at the NEC. From there things just went from strength to strength. Over the last year or so I've got to know Ted well and I like to think we've grown into good friends. He's shown himself to be a very dependable young man and we've all been immensely impressed by the additional support he's given his mum since her sad loss. I only met Arthur twice, but that was enough to convince me that he was as happy at the prospects of his son's marriage as I was at my daughter's. So we can rejoice today that Arthur's hopes and wishes for his son have been realised.

It is customary for the bride's father to offer the newlyweds some profound piece of advice – advice that's been passed down from generation to generation and no doubt ignored by all of them. So instead I'll simply say to you both: Have a good life. I mean that. Ladies and Gentlemen, please stand, raise your glasses, and drink with me a toast to the health and happiness of Ted and Carol.

Ted and Carol!

(Where both the bride and bridegroom have recently lost a parent adapt and personalise the relevant parts of speeches 3 and 4.)

Model speech 5: Bride's mother
Formal reception – where the bride was brought up in a single-parent family.

Reverend Goodman, Ladies and Gentlemen, Dora just asked me, 'Would you like to speak now or should we let our guests enjoy themselves a little longer?' She always has had a way with words.

What a joy it is to see so many happy faces here today – and none happier than those of this young couple. And why not? Bryan has married Dora and Dora is gaining Bryan and losing me.

I was so proud to see Dora today as she swept down the aisle. Proud and surprised – I'd never seen her sweep anything before. But seriously, no one could have asked for more from a daughter. She deserves happiness and with Bryan I am confident she has found it.

Bryan is a very hard-working lad and we are all very proud of his recent success with his NVQs. When he asked me for Dora's hand, I asked, 'Bryan, do you think you're earning enough to support a family?' 'Yes,' he replied. 'Think very carefully now,' I added, 'after all, you know there are five of us.' Only joking, Bryan. But I do want you to know you really are one of the family now.

Of course from time to time there will be problems, but I cannot imagine two people better equipped to face them. So I ask you all to be upstanding, to raise your glasses and to drink to the health and happiness of Dora and Bryan.

To Dora and Bryan!

Model speech 6: Close family friend, relative or godfather

Formal reception — where the bride was brought up in a
single-parent family and her mother (or father) does not want
to speak.

Ladies and Gentlemen, I'm very honoured that Kylie's mother/father, Pat, asked me to propose a toast to the happy couple. I have known Kylie for many years and I have spent several pleasurable evenings watching her acting with the Plymouth Players. Well today there is no doubt that she is the star of the show – well, co-star anyway, alongside Jason.

I've got to know Jason well over the last few months and he's proved himself to be a very dependable, friendly and hard-working young man. Not only does he have a good job, but he is wisely continuing his education at night school. So, all being well, he should become a fully qualified chartered accountant within three years.

I am confident that Kylie and Jason have all the qualities needed to build a strong and successful marriage. They both have the sense of humour, love and support for one another necessary to help them through any difficult times, and the courage and determination to make sure things soon go right again. So let us raise our glasses and drink to the health and happiness of Kylie and Jason.

To Kylie and Jason!

Model speech 7: Bride's father

Formal reception – where the bridegroom was brought up in a single-parent family.

Ladies and Gentlemen, what an historic day this is! This very day, the 1st of June, will always be associated with three world-famous events. Screen legend Marilyn Monroe was born in 1926, The Beatles released the classic *Sergeant Pepper's Lonely Hearts Club Band* in 1967, and on this day in 200X, Andrew married Myfanwy!

Thank you all so much for coming to celebrate this happy day. What a joy it is to see so many happy faces, and none more radiant than those of the young people on my right. Marriage, they say, is made in heaven. Well I'm afraid I beg to disagree. This marriage was not made in heaven, it was made at my retirement party when I introduced Andy to Myfanwy. I hasten to add that it was early retirement. Later that evening I remember my wife, Jean, commenting that they seemed to be getting on rather well. To be honest, I didn't take much notice at the time but four months later, when Andy asked my advice on engagement rings, I knew she was right.

And from that moment Myfanwy hardly stopped planning and arranging things to make sure everything went as smoothly as it did today. Even yesterday I overheard her say to her mother, 'Mum, I've still got so much to do and I want everything to be perfect. I'm determined not to overlook even the most insignificant detail.' And her mother replying, 'Don't worry, I'll make sure your father is there.'

Myfanwy is the best daughter any parents could have asked for. And if I'm accused of being biased, then I plead guilty – and proud of it. But everyone has faults – even Myfanwy. Andy, occasionally she is a little economical with the truth – but that is all she is economical with. For example, she certainly hasn't been economical with all the love and kindness she has displayed to her parents.

I worked with Andy for three years so I know him well. Our boss called him a miracle worker because it was a miracle if he worked. No, it's because I know Andy so well that I know I can get away with a crack like that. He has a great sense of humour and he really is a very hardworking young man. I know I'm not breaking any confidences when I tell you how proud his mother, June, is that he has decided to enrol for an Open University degree course.

As tradition demands, I shall pass on to you both one pearl of wisdom about the institution of marriage – it is the kind of advice you might expect from a former financial adviser: Marriage is an investment that pays dividends so long as you take the time to pay interest – and that's more than mere speculation.

I know, and you know, that these young people are going to be blissfully happy. Let us stand up, and raise our glasses and drink a toast to the health and happiness of Andy and Myfanwy.

To Andy and Myfanwy!

(Where both the bride and bridegroom were brought up in single-parent families adapt and personalise the relevant parts of speeches 6 and 7.)

We now must consider the thorny subject of speeches at second (and subsequent) weddings. Some people believe it best to make absolutely no reference to previous marriages. However, this tactic can backfire – especially if any of their children are present. For this reason others prefer to stop any gossipers in their tracks by being quite open about this aspect of their pasts. Why not ask the couple how they would like you to play it? If they want you to take the second approach, model speeches 8 to 10 should help.

Model speech 8: Bride's father

Formal reception or informal wedding party – where the bride has been married before.

Richard, for you this is a first marriage and a time of hope and excitement. For Elizabeth it is a second marriage. You are truly honoured. Despite all the difficulties of her first marriage, she decided she simply had to try again. You must have had some effect on her. This is a new start and, if you will forgive the cliché, today really is the first day of the rest of your lives. We all wish you everything that you wish yourselves and I would now like to propose a toast to your health and happiness.

To Richard and Elizabeth!

Model speech 9: Bride's father

Formal reception or informal wedding party – where the bridegroom has been married before.

Anne, for you this is a first marriage and a time of hope and anticipation. For Henry it is a second marriage. When he met you he decided that he simply had to marry again despite the difficulties of his first attempt. Anne, you must have had some effect on him. And think of it this way: the man you are marrying has already had the sharp corners rubbed off and he is already house-trained, so you won't have to bother with sandpaper or a litter tray.

But seriously, we sincerely hope you will always enjoy life together. This is a new start and, as they say, it is the first day of the rest of your lives. So let's raise our glasses and drink a toast to the health and happiness of Anne and Henry.

To Anne and Henry!

Model speech 10: Bride's father, close family friend or relative

Formal reception or informal wedding party – where both parties have been divorced or widowed at least once.

(Obviously, you will need to word your speech carefully, according to whether the parties have been widowed and/or divorced, and how long ago this happened.)

Ladies and Gentlemen, all marriages are special occasions but a second marriage is an unsurpassable event because no one goes into it looking through rose-tinted glasses. You know what kind of problems must be faced and what sort of mistakes must be avoided. And, of course, it is impossible to avoid such pitfalls until you first know they are there.

It cannot be easy later in life to put away the past and begin again but we know you have all the qualities needed to make this new chapter of your lives a great success. Everyone has the right to happiness — the grandmother as much as the granddaughter.

So we are all delighted that your times of loneliness and sadness are behind you. This is another chance to find true happiness; a time of renewed hope. And it is an honour for us to be here to share this new beginning with you. We are confident that you will now receive all the joy you so richly deserve. I know I speak for everyone present when I say we wish you all the very best for a wonderful future together. Ladies and Gentlemen, please join me in a toast to the health and happiness of Joan and Peter.

To Joan and Peter!

While we are considering potentially tricky situations, we must think about the kind of things you should say where the couple already have at least one child. Once again, it's best to ask them first, but a short, light, slightly humorous speech is safest.

Model speech 11: Bride's father

Formal reception or informal wedding party – where the couple already has at least one child.

Ladies and Gentlemen, marriage is an institution – but who wants to live in an institution? Well, here are two young people who have decided that their lives will be even happier in this institution – and we are delighted that they have.

For most people marriage is a bit of a lottery. Sometimes they find that the person they have married doesn't seem to be the same person they were engaged to. Bob and Paula don't need to worry about this. They know each other so well by now that they are certain their marriage will be a success. In many ways they have been far more sensible than the majority of us in finding this out before they tied the knot.

A successful marriage involves falling in love many, many times – but each time with the same person. We know Bob and Paula will continue to do this and will make sure that little Jodie is brought up in a strong, loving family unit – which is exactly how it should be. I was going to wish you both the best of luck for the future, but you have already proved that you don't need luck. So instead I will invite everyone to join me in a toast. Ladies and Gentlemen, let us drink to the health and happiness of Bob and Paula.

To Bob and Paula!

But perhaps only one of the couple is already a parent. Ask them if they want you to be open about this in your speech. If they do, you could say something similar to model speech 12.

Model speech 12: Bride's father

Formal reception or informal wedding party – where the bridegroom already has at least one child.

Ladies and Gentlemen, this is an historic day! This day, the 14th of March, will always be associated with three truly momentous events. The Russian Revolution ended in 1917; Michael Caine was born in 1933 (not a lot of people know that); and on this day in 200X, Mike married Sarah!

You know, it seems just like yesterday when I came home and found little Sarah grooming the dog. 'Don't worry,' she said, 'I'll put your toothbrush back in the bathroom afterwards, like I always do.' Well, from today she won't need my toothbrush because now she's got her very own groom.

During the time I've known Mike, I like to think we've become friends. At the same time Martha and I have also become great friends with his parents, Tom and Barbara. Then, of course, there is little Wendy. And who could not fall for her? But you know you can't fool kids. They are true judges of character and they tell it like it is. So I am absolutely delighted that Wendy loves Sarah as much as Sarah so clearly loves her.

I am reminded of a quotation by Bertrand Russell – reminded, that is, by Martha who looked it up last night: 'Of all forms of caution, caution in love is perhaps the most fatal to true happiness.' I am delighted that Sarah and Mike have thrown caution to the wind. Mike is a man who knows where he is going in life and I am confident he is the right man for Sarah.

So can I ask you all to stand, raise your glasses, and drink a toast with me to the health and happiness of Sarah and Mike.

To Sarah and Mike!

Model speech 13: Bride's father

Formal reception or informal wedding party – where the bride already has at least one child.

Ladies and Gentlemen, 'Some talk of Alexander, and some of Hercules, and Hector and Lysander and such great names as these.' But I would rather talk about Sergeant and Mrs Wilson – about Terry and June.

June has been the best daughter any parents could have asked for – she is beautiful, charming, intelligent and, well, perfect in every way. She does everything for me – she even wrote this speech. Terry, June does admit to having one or two small faults but she insists that ever being wrong isn't one of them. And you certainly weren't wrong in choosing her.

I've known Terry for over two years now and he has proved himself to be a reliable, hard-working young man. And he gets on brilliantly with young David. You know you can't fool kids. They are true judges of character. And if they don't like you they won't pretend they do. Well, David does like Terry – very much indeed. And I know the feeling is reciprocal.

Bob Hope once said, 'Marriage is an institution and no family should be without one.' How I agree. Quite simply, Terry and

June make a perfect match. So I ask you all to join me in drinking a toast to their health and happiness.

To Terry and June!

Model speech 14: Bride's father

Informal wedding party.

Ladies and Gentlemen, thank you for coming to celebrate this happiest of days. I would like to propose a toast to the happy couple, Pamela and Billy. May they enjoy good fortune, continued good health and immense happiness in their future together. May problems follow them all their lives – and never catch up with them.

To Pamela and Billy!

Model speech 15: A close family friend, relative or godfather

Informal wedding party – where the bride's father is present but does not make a speech.

Friends, I am honoured to have been asked to say a few words on this happy occasion. We all know that Judy and Richard are such fun-loving people [*or talented, lively, warm-hearted, generous, or clever people*] and that they are certain to bring the best out in one another. We wish them a long and happy marriage together and I ask you now to raise your glasses and drink to Judy and Richard.

To Judy and Richard!

Model speech 16: A close family friend, relative or godfather

Informal wedding party — where the bride's father is recently deceased.

Friends, it gives me special pleasure to be present at the wedding of my good friends Alf and Else. This is a lovely, small, intimate gathering of friends, which is just the way the happy couple wanted it. We all have personal knowledge of Alf's loyal friendship and kindness and we are delighted that he has married Else who is equally admired and respected for her qualities of generosity and warm-heartedness. How proud Arthur would have been of her today. Doesn't she look wonderful? I know how much Arthur was looking forward to this day and in a way, I feel we're making this speech together. Let's all rejoice that his wishes for his daughter's happiness have now come true. So will you join me in drinking a toast to Alf and Else?

To Alf and Else!

Model speech 17: Bride's father

Informal wedding party – where one of the bridegroom's parents is recently deceased.

Ladies and Gentlemen, thank you all so much for joining my daughter, Alice and my new son, Danny, as they celebrate their first day of married life together. Few words are necessary because you know them both so well. You know what a determined young lady Alice is and how proud Rosemary and I are of her recent promotion. And you know what a charming, humorous and hard-working young man Danny is and how proud his dad, Frank, was of him. In a sense

I feel he is celebrating here with his wife, Betty, because, like me, Frank believed they were made for each other. So let's raise our glasses and drink to Alice and Danny.

To Alice and Danny!

(Where both the bride and bridegroom have recently lost a parent adapt and personalise the relevant parts of speeches 16 and 17.)

Model speech 18: Bride's mother
Informal wedding party – where the bride was brought up in a single-parent family.

Ladies and Gentlemen – Friends, I would like to propose a toast to the best daughter in the world and to the man who has been her husband for [*look at your watch*], for 58½ minutes – precisely. I am confident that they have a bright future together. I'm not losing a daughter, I'm gaining a son. So I ask you all to raise your glasses and to drink to their health and happiness.

To Susan and George!

Model speech 19: A close family friend, relative or godfather
Informal wedding party – where the bride was brought up in a single-parent family and her mother (or father) does not want to speak.

I am very honoured that Mary has asked me to propose a toast to the happy couple. We all know Wilma and Fred as fun-loving people [*or generous, or warm-hearted people*] who are sure to bring the best out in one another. They deserve the very best, so let's wish them a long and happy married life together.

Has everyone got a drink? Good.

To Wilma and Fred!

Model speech 20: Bride's father

Informal wedding party – where the bridegroom was brought up in a single-parent family.

Friends, today has been a very happy day for all of us, and nobody in this room looks happier than the young couple sitting there. Obviously I know Esther very well and I can tell you, Desmond, you have made a very wise choice. Over the last year or so I've also got to know Desmond and his delightful mother, Rebecca, and I can tell you, Esther, you've made an equally wise choice. You were both made for each other.

Have you all got a drink? Good. Let's drink a toast to Esther and Desmond.

To Esther and Desmond!

(Where both the bride and bridegroom were brought up in single-parent families adapt and personalise the relevant parts of speeches 19 and 20.)

Model speech 21: Best man

Informal wedding party with no bridesmaids.

I am very honoured, as I'm sure you are, to be here among this select little gathering today. We are all close friends or relatives of the happy couple, which is exactly how Tom and Jenny wanted it. Few words are necessary because you all already know of Jenny's unique qualities of kindness, loyalty and friendship. And we all admire the way Tom has worked so hard to get his new business off the ground. We wish him well. So all I will say is that I know I speak for you all when I say we are absolutely delighted that they have decided to tie the knot. Quite simply, they were meant for each other. So let's raise our glasses and drink to their health and happiness.

To Tom and Jenny!

RESPONDING TO THE TOAST AND PROPOSING A SECOND TOAST

The bridegroom responds to the toast to the bride and bridegroom making it clear he is speaking on behalf of both of them (unless his bride is going to speak as well – see speech 38). You must convey that you are conscious of the meaning of the occasion and its importance to you. It is really a general thank you speech. You thank the previous speaker for his or her kind words, your parents and your wife's for being such wonderful parents, the gathering for their good wishes and gifts, and all those who have helped to make the wedding ceremony and reception such successes. You then say some nice things about the bridesmaids before proposing a toast to them. If there are no bridesmaids and no maid/matron of honour, the toast is to your parents-in-law (see speech 40).

The speech should be very sentimental and should include the right balance of humour and seriousness. There is no hard and fast rule about what this balance should be. It really comes down to common sense. For example, if the bride or bridegroom was brought up in a single-parent family, it would be inappropriate to talk at any length about the sanctity of the institution of marriage. So, to a large extent, the content of your speech should reflect and be in tone with your background and personal circumstances, and with those of your wife.

Model speech 22: Bridegroom's reply

Formal reception.

Reverend Green, Ladies and Gentlemen, we are told that marriage is a lottery. Well if it is, then I have hit the jackpot. Quite simply, I'm the luckiest man in the world to have a wife like Karen and to have friends like you to join us on this our happiest day. Happiest day so far that is because in the words of Karen's favourite Carpenters' song, 'We've only just begun. So much of life ahead. A kiss for luck [*blow her a kiss*] and we're on our way.' Yes Karen, we've only just begun.

But I've been lucky in so many other ways as well. Lucky in having the best parents in the world. Parents who knew that the most important thing they could do for their children was to love each other. Lucky in my new parents-in-law. What a horrible expression that is – parents-in-law. Let's call them parents-by-marriage. I'd like to thank them for giving us such a lovely wedding and reception, and, even more, for producing a daughter like Karen. And no one could have been luckier in their choice of best man. Doesn't he look terrific? I know he won't mind if I let you into a little secret – Alec always wears that suit when he goes to our monthly rugby social evenings. As we left for church this morning his five-year-old son, Christian, grabbed him by the sleeve and asked why he was wearing it today when he knew it always gave him such a headache the next morning.

But let's face it, Karen is a very lucky lady too. No, I don't mean because she married me, although I suppose she could have done worse. No, I mean because today she too has gained two wonderful parents-by-marriage. And she is lucky in the support she has received from her charming bridesmaids. I know how helpful they have been to Karen, not only today but in those long weeks of preparation that brides go in for. So before I sit down I ask you to join me in showing your gratitude to Tracy, Sharon and Dorien by offering them a toast.

Ladies and Gentlemen, the bridesmaids!

Model speech 23: Bridegroom's reply

Formal reception – where the bride's father is recently deceased.

Ladies and Gentlemen, my wife and I [*pause for laughter and applause*] would like to thank you all for your generous gifts. I cannot imagine a happier way to start married life than with our friends and family around us, but you really have been ridiculously over-generous with your gifts.

I have a few personal thank-yous to make too. George, I do not deserve the good things you have said of me – but I will try to deserve them, and to be worthy of my wife. Oh, how proud Henry would have been of Clare today. Doesn't she look wonderful? Thank you, Victoria, for allowing me to marry your beautiful daughter and for arranging this magnificent reception. And thanks also to my own parents.

Both Clare and I have been very fortunate having grown up knowing the real meaning of marriage through the example of our parents.

Then of course I must thank James for being best man, though I'm not sure how thankful to be because I haven't heard his speech yet. And a special word of thanks is due to Hans and Gretel, my dear friends who have travelled all the way from Holland to be with us today. Hans, I've got a couple of bottles of schnapps in. Thank you both so much for coming – *dank U wel.*

Finally, what can I say about the bridesmaids, the charming young ladies who did such a great job in helping Clare up the aisle – although I hope she came to the church of her own free will. They have been wonderful and have added so much to the occasion, so please join me in drinking a toast to Victoria, Petunia, Primrose and Zinnia.

Ladies and Gentlemen, the bridesmaids!

Model speech 24: Bridegroom's reply

Formal reception – where one of his parents is recently deceased.

Ladies and Gentlemen, thank you all so much for coming to our wedding and for being so generous with all your gifts. Carol will certainly find the lawn mower and electric drill useful and I will make full use of the deck chairs and the portable TV. Only joking, Carol. I'd like to take this opportunity to make a few personal thank-yous too. Martin, thank you for those kind words – but why didn't you give me your tip for the National? [*This reference to the National shows the bridegroom was listening to the first speaker – and responding to what he said – because it was not in his draft speech.*] And thanks to you and Gail for producing a daughter such as Carol, and for laying on this wonderful reception. Thanks too to my mother simply for being my mother. Mum, Dad loved Carol almost as much as I do – *almost* as much. And how I agree with Martin that we can rejoice in the fact that the marriage he so much wanted has now taken place. [*Another unrehearsed response to the earlier speech.*] In a sense, I feel he is celebrating with us.

A special word of thanks is due to our attendants. My best man, Carl, is a man of hidden talents. I just hope that one day he'll find them. No, thanks Carl, you did a great job today. And so did these charming young bridesmaids. Don't they look a picture? Ladies and Gentlemen, will you please join me in drinking a toast to the bridesmaids?

The bridesmaids!

(Where both the bride and groom have recently lost a parent adapt and personalise the relevant parts of speeches 23 and 24.)

Model speech 25: Bridegroom's reply
Formal reception – where the bride was brought up in a single-parent family.

Reverend Goodman, Ladies and Gentlemen, thanks for those kind words, Mum. My wife and I [*pause*], oh how I've waited to say those words. My wife and I are delighted that you were able to come to our wedding. I can't imagine a happier way to start married life than with our families and friends around us. And thank you all so much for your gifts. With all these saucepans and toasters it looks like I'm going to have to get used to boiled toast. But seriously, we do sincerely thank you for the wonderful gifts you have given us.

I have a couple of personal thank-yous to make, too. I am especially grateful to Mary, my new mother-in-law, for helping arrange this reception and even more for bringing up Dora so well that she has become the lady you see before you today.

And, of course, thanks to my parents for their contribution to today's festivities and for teaching me the difference between right and wrong, so I know which I'm enjoying at any particular time. Thanks must also go to Ian, my best man, who got me to the church on time.

I am also delighted that Auntie Hilda and Uncle Horace managed to make the long journey from Glasgow to be with us here today. Did you take the high road or the low road? Finally my sincere thanks go to the bridesmaids. They were wonderful and so well behaved. I know you will want to join me in drinking a toast to the delightful young ladies who supported Dora so well on her big day.

Ladies and Gentlemen, the bridesmaids!

Model speech 26: Bridegroom's reply

Formal reception – where he was brought up in a single-parent family.

Ladies and Gentlemen, my wife and I [*pause*] are so pleased you are here to share what is the happiest day of our lives – so far. Thank you so much for your wonderful gifts – they really are exactly what we needed. I hope to get round to thanking you all personally later.

But first I would like to say a few other thank-yous. First and foremost to Flo: thank you for marrying me. And thanks to her parents for making me feel like one of the family – and, of course, for arranging this wonderful gathering. Thanks, too, to my mother. In the fullness of time, if I am half as good at being one parent as my mother has been at being two, I will have succeeded beyond my wildest expectations.

And doesn't Radha look a picture – a real dandy. But I'll let you into a secret: he borrowed that suit from me. To be fair, he had ordered one but the trousers had to be altered. Yesterday they told him they wouldn't be ready in time. So he's going to sue them for promise of breeches. Now it is my duty – no, my pleasure – to propose a toast to the bridesmaids. They all did their jobs magnificently. Please stand, raise your glasses, and drink a toast to the bridesmaids.

The bridesmaids!

(Where both the bride and bridegroom were brought up in single-parent families adapt and personalise the relevant parts of speeches 25 and 26.)

We must now consider the situations where the bridegroom and/or the bride have been married before. Some people decide to make no reference to this whatsoever, while others are quite open about it. It is entirely up to you. However, if you decide to take the first option, make sure that the person who proposes the opening toast, and your best man, are not going to say anything about it either. On the other hand, if you choose the second option, speeches 27 to 29 should help.

Model speech 27: Bridegroom's reply

Formal reception or informal wedding party – where the bride has been married before.

Ladies and Gentlemen – Friends, I would like to say a few sincere thank-yous. First, thank you all for coming to our wedding, for your good wishes and for your most generous gifts. And of course thank you, Elizabeth, for taking me on. I promise that for you this will be second time lucky. Thanks also to Charles for those wise words. Yes, I am honoured. [*This was said in response to the first speaker – it was not in the draft speech.*] And thanks to you and Camilla for accepting me so readily into your family and also for laying on this wonderful reception/party. Then how could I forget my parents? Thanks Mam and Dad for everything you have done for me over the years. I will always be grateful. Always. And what about that dashing young man over there. Steve, thank you for making sure everything ran so smoothly today. And finally, I must say a word about the bridesmaids. They were charming and so elegant in everything they did. So please join me in a toast to the bridesmaids.

Ladies and Gentlemen, the bridesmaids!

Model speech 28: Bridegroom's reply

Formal reception or informal wedding party – where the bridegroom has been married before.

Ladies and Gentlemen, thank you so much for attending our wedding and for all these splendid gifts. I would like to offer a few personal thank-yous as well. First and foremost, thank you, Anne, for marrying me. This time I am not marrying for better or for worse — I am marrying for good. And thanks to your parents for producing such a beautiful daughter and for arranging this wonderful reception/party. Thanks, too, to my parents – not least for having me. And also to Zack for getting me to the church on time. Finally, my thanks must go to the charming young ladies who did such a great job in helping Anne up the aisle. Please join me in a toast to the bridesmaids.

Ladies and Gentlemen, the bridesmaids!

Model speech 29: Bridegroom's reply

Formal reception or informal wedding party – where both parties have been divorced or widowed at least once.

(You will need to word your speech very carefully, according to whether you and your wife have been widowed and/or divorced, and also how long ago this happened.)

Thank you, James, for those wise words. Joan and I know how lucky we are to have this second chance in life and we have decided to grab it with both hands. In the words of the old song, 'We're not so old, and not so plain, and we're quite prepared to marry again'. Whatever we may have said during the wedding ceremony, we are not marrying for better or worse — we are marrying for good.

My wife and I [*pause*] want to thank you all for coming to our wedding today, and for your lovely gifts. A particular word of thanks is due to James and Joyce for laying on this wonderful reception/party. Next, I must thank Rolf, who was undoubtedly the best man to get me to the church on time. And finally, my thanks go to Ena, Martha and Minnie, those charming young ladies who did such a wonderful job today. Ladies and Gentlemen, will you now all join me in drinking a toast to the bridesmaids?

Ladies and Gentlemen, the bridesmaids!

But what if you already have one or more children? You may decide not to make any reference to this in your speech. However, this could seem a little odd, because the guests are certain to already know about your child(ren). Whatever you decide, make sure all the other speech makers know precisely how you want them to play it so none of them will say anything out of turn. If you do decide to refer to your family, the following is the sort of thing you should say.

Model speech 30: Bridegroom's reply

Formal reception or informal wedding party – where the couple already have at least one child.

Thank you for those kind words. My wife and I [*pause*] are delighted you came to our wedding. As they say, better late than never. You see we needed a new toaster and a few saucepans and as Argos was closed . . .

I'd like to take this opportunity to say a few personal thank-yous. First and foremost to Paula for marrying me. To her parents for being such great people and for arranging this wonderful reception/party. To my parents for being the best parents in the world. To Robin for being my best man and my best friend. And finally, to the most charming set of bridesmaids I have ever seen – Rita, Audrey, Vera and our lovely daughter, Jodie. So will you all kindly stand and drink a toast to these delightful bridesmaids.

Ladies and Gentlemen, the bridesmaids!

But perhaps only one of you is already a parent. If you decide not to make any reference to this, make sure nobody else is going to either. However, if you are going to be quite open about it, speeches 31 and 32 should be of help.

Model speech 31: Bridegroom's reply

Formal reception or informal wedding party – where he already has a child.

Ladies and Gentlemen, my wife and I [*pause*] thank you all for your generous gifts. I'd like to add a few personal thank-yous, too. To Sarah's parents, George and Martha, for laying on this wonderful reception/wedding party and, even more, for producing Sarah. George, thank you for those wise words. I do not deserve the good things you said of me, but I shall try to deserve them, and be worthy of my family – my daughter, Wendy, and her mother, Sarah. Thanks, too, to my parents for being so supportive over the years. You could not have done more. And thank you, Ken, for getting me to the church on time. But my greatest thanks must go to Sarah – for marrying me.

It is my final duty – no, pleasure – to thank the bridesmaids for helping Sarah up the aisle. Don't they look a picture? Will you all join me in drinking a toast to them?

Ladies and Gentlemen, the bridesmaids!

Model speech 32: Bridegroom's reply

Formal reception or informal wedding party – where his wife already has a child.

Ladies and Gentlemen, thank you, Peter, for those wise words. My wife and I [*pause*] would like to thank you all for coming to our wedding and for your most generous gifts. I'd like to take this opportunity to add a few personal thank-yous too. Thanks to June's parents, Peter and Sandra, for arranging this wonderful reception/wedding party and, of course, for arranging June. Thanks to my parents, Nick and Sue, for everything they have done for me over the years – far too much for me to even begin to describe here today. Thank you. And thanks to Alan for being the best best man a bridegroom could have hoped for. But most of all, thanks to June for taking me on. I will try my hardest to be a worthy husband and father.

Finally, what can I say about that delightful set of bridesmaids over there? They were magnificent. Please join me in drinking a toast to them.

Ladies and Gentlemen, the bridesmaids!

Model speech 33: Bridegroom's reply

Informal wedding party.

Ladies and Gentlemen – Friends, my wife and I [*pause*] want to say a sincere thank-you for coming to our wedding and for being so generous with your presents. And I want to say thank you on my own behalf to Kylie for taking me on, to her parents for producing such a wonderful daughter, to my parents for being so supportive to me over the years, and to my best man,

John, who made sure everything ran so smoothly. I have one final duty – no, it is not a duty, it is a genuine pleasure. I have the pleasure of proposing a toast to the health of the young ladies who supported Kylie so magnificently today.

Ladies and Gentlemen, the bridesmaids!

Model speech 34: Bridegroom's reply

Informal wedding party – where the bride's father is recently deceased.

Ladies and Gentlemen, my wife and I [*pause*] are delighted that you found the time to join us here today. It has made such a difference to have been surrounded by our closest friends on this, our big day. We have been overwhelmed by your kindness and generosity. Jenny's mother has been wonderful. We all know what a very difficult time she has been through recently but she insisted on helping with all our preparations and I am sure that her daughter's wedding will have provided a bright light in what must have otherwise been a very dark year for her. Margaret, thank you so much for all your support. I can promise you that you haven't lost a daughter, you've gained a son. They say a girl grows up to be like her mother – well I can only hope it's true.

And I mustn't forget my parents. Their help, like Margaret's, has been above and beyond the call of duty.

Then there is Geraint, my best man. We met at university and I can tell you that those of you who don't know him are the luckiest people in the world – because the pleasure of getting to know him lies ahead of you.

Finally, I must mention the bridesmaids who have done so much to help my wife. Don't they look a picture? Let's all drink a toast to them.

Ladies and Gentlemen, the bridesmaids!

Model speech 35: Bridegroom's reply

Informal wedding party – where one of his parents is recently deceased.

Thank you, Bruce, for those kind words. My wife and I [*pause*] are delighted you could all make it to our wedding today. And thank you so much for your generous gifts. I hope to be able to thank you all personally later. Thanks, too, to Alice's mum and dad, Bruce and Rosemary, for allowing me to marry their beautiful daughter and for arranging this magnificent party. And thanks, of course, must also go to my mum who has done so much for me – much more than I could possibly begin to tell you about here. And dad was so much looking forward to today that I agree, Bruce, in a special sort of way he's sitting here with us with that wicked smile on his face, joining in with all the toasts. [*Obviously, this was a response to something said in an earlier speech and it was not in his draft.*]

I would also like to thank Desmond for being such an efficient best man. Although I'm not sure how thankful to be because I haven't heard his speech yet.

Finally, thanks to these delightful young ladies who have done a great job in helping Alice up the aisle – although I hope she came to the church of her own free will. So will you all stand and join me in drinking a toast to the bridesmaids?

Ladies and Gentlemen, the bridesmaids!

(Where both the bride and bridegroom have recently lost a parent adapt and personalise the relevant parts of speeches 34 and 35.)

Model speech 36: Bridegroom's reply
Informal wedding party – where the bride was brought up in a single-parent family.

Ladies and Gentlemen, you may not realise it but this is a truly historic day. This day, the 16th of May, will always be remembered because of three world-famous events. The first Oscars were awarded in 1929; singer Janet Jackson was born in 1966; and on this day in 200X, I married Michelle!

My wife and I [*pause*] want to thank you all for attending this little gathering and for your very useful gifts. I would also like to offer a few personal thank-yous. To Beth, my new mother-in-law, for bringing up her daughter to become the charming, witty and considerate lady I was fortunate enough to marry today. To my parents, Jayne and Christopher, for having me – and for much, much more than that. To Branwell for being the best best man a groom could hope for. And to Charlotte, Emily and Ann for being such delightful bridesmaids. In fact, I think we should drink a toast to them, don't you?

Ladies and Gentlemen, the bridesmaids!

Model speech 37: Bridegroom's reply

Informal wedding party – where he was brought up in a single-parent family.

Thank you, Gavin, for those kind words. My wife and I [*pause*] would like to thank you all for attending our wedding and for your most generous gifts and good wishes. If I could also add one or two personal thank-yous . . . Thank you to Esther's parents, Gavin and Ruth, for so readily accepting me as one of their family. To my mother, Rebecca, for being the best mum in the world. To Howard for not losing the ring. And to the charming bridesmaids, Isra and Caroline, for doing such a magnificent job today. Will you all join me in drinking a toast to them?

Ladies and Gentlemen, the bridesmaids!

(Where both the bride and bridegroom were brought up in single-parent families adapt and personalise the relevant parts of speeches 36 and 37.)

It is not necessary for the bride to make a speech, but if she wants to the number and order of speeches will need to be revised, perhaps to:

1. Toast to the bride and groom by the bride's father.

2. Response by the bridegroom (omitting the toast to the bridesmaids).

3. Response by the bride.

4. Toast to the bridesmaids by a close friend, relative or godfather.

5. Response by the best man.

What follows is the sort of thing the bride should say:

Model speech 38: Bride's response

Formal reception or informal wedding party.

Ladies and Gentlemen, I'm very glad to break with tradition and say a few words of my own on this happy occasion. This is the happiest day in my life since I was in the arms of another woman's husband – my mother's. Mum told me the only time a woman really succeeds in changing a man is when he's a baby – so I still have time to change Shane. Thank you all for your generous gifts, thanks to Shane's parents for making me feel I am their daughter, and to my parents for more than I could ever begin to tell. Thank you.

Model speech 39: Bridegroom's reply

Formal reception or informal wedding party – where there are no bridesmaids, but there is a maid/matron of honour.

Ladies and Gentlemen, my wife and I [*pause*] thank you all so much for coming to our wedding and for bringing these wonderful gifts. We would particularly like to thank our parents for all the support they have given us over the years and our mothers in particular for arranging this superb reception/party. Our thanks also must go to Damian, my best man, and to Marlene, Kelly's maid of honour. They were magnificent. In fact, would you join me and drink a toast to Damian and Marlene?

Ladies and Gentlemen, to Damian and Marlene!

Where there are no bridesmaids and no maid/matron of honour, the toast is to your parents-in-law.

Model speech 40: Bridegroom's reply

Formal reception or informal wedding party – where there are no bridesmaids and no maid/matron of honour.

Ladies and Gentlemen, my wife and I [*pause*] are delighted you were able to join us on this, our happiest day. It goes almost without saying what a difference it makes to have our closest friends here with us. Thank you so much for your kind wishes and your wonderful presents. Thanks also to Jayne's parents for making me really feel like one of the family – which of course I now am – and to my parents for everything they have done for me over the years. Finally, my thanks go to Jimmy for not losing the ring.

I cannot begin to tell you how happy Jenny and I are today. I wish the whole world could be feeling the same way and I hope you all enjoy a wonderful afternoon/evening. Please raise your glasses and join me in drinking a toast to our generous hosts, two wonderful people, my new parents-in-law, George and Mildred.

To George and Mildred!

RESPONDING ON BEHALF OF THE BRIDESMAIDS

Rather oddly, it is traditional for the best man to respond to the toast to the bridesmaids. All that is required is acknowledgement of the toast, and a few light-hearted and humorous words about the bridegroom – with a couple of compliments and congratulatory remarks woven in.

While you could also tell a joke or two against yourself, *never* say a single word against the bride or her mother (although a teasing remark about the bride's *job* or *hobby* would not be out of place). A little flippancy is fine, but you must avoid anything that could be considered too risqué, offensive or cynical. Also steer well clear of any emotional or serious issues – such weighty matters are the prerogative of the bride's father and the bridegroom.

Don't just string a series of jokes together either – you are not a stand-up comedian. Your overall purpose is to respond to the toast to the bridesmaids and to return a few sincere congratulatory remarks to the happy couple. The best way to do this in an amusing and entertaining manner is to sugar some teasing remarks with a few sincere words of praise and compliments.

Because this is a very jokey, upbeat speech, the backgrounds and circumstances of the bride and bridegroom (from a single-parent family; parent recently deceased; married before, and so on) are largely irrelevant, although obviously you must take care to avoid saying anything insensitive. For example, if the groom's father died of a coronary, don't say he had a heart of gold.

If you are the final speaker, signal this by reading the tele-messages immediately after finishing your speech (having first checked that they are not X-rated). If there are to be more speeches (see speeches 49 and 50), stand up, pointedly look at the clock, and read the messages after the final speaker to ensure he really *is* the final speaker.

Try to keep the tele-message session interesting by giving a few background details about the contents of the messages and about the people who sent them. Crack a joke if the moment seems right. As always, aim to end on a particularly high note. You could end with the funniest or most emotional message, or with one from some relatives who live on the other side of the world, or perhaps with one from some very old family friends (in both senses of the phrase). Alternatively, you could simply *make up* the last message. However, if you do this, you must make it obvious to everyone that this is a joke: 'And finally, this is from the writer who created *Jeeves and Wooster* – P.G. Wodehouse. It says, "All unhappy marriages are a result of the husband having brains". I have total confidence this marriage will be an exceptionally happy one.'

Model speech 41: Best man's reply

Formal reception – Example 1.

Ladies and Gentlemen, thank you, Kevin, for those kind words about the bridesmaids and attendants. It has been a pleasure for all of us to be a small part of your big day. And what about the dresses chosen by Sally and her mother Denise? They have attracted so much favourable comment from the guests here that I have to give them a special mention. [*Pause for cries of 'Hear, hear'.*] [*This reference to their dresses obviously was not in his draft speech.*]

Before I say a word or two about our groom, I must admit that I have made a very similar little speech about Kevin twice before – once to the Ashford's Arsonists' Association and once to the Clitheroe's Clog-dancers Club. So I apologise to those of you who may have already heard it once before.

And to those of you who have already heard it twice, please don't burn my shoes.

As Max Bygraves used to say, I wanna tell you a story, because I think it sums up nicely the kind of man Sally has married. Soon after we met, Kevin invited me to his eighteenth birthday party. At the time I knew hardly anyone in Manchester – in fact I was getting a bit depressed with life. Kevin didn't really know me either – I was an acquaintance of a friend of a friend. But despite this he absolutely insisted I came to his do. He wouldn't take no for an answer and he almost forced details of his address upon me. For the first time since I moved here, I felt wanted.

He said, 'A number 23 bus will bring you right to my door – 9 Rosamond Street. Walk up to the front door and press the doorbell with your elbow.' 'Why my elbow, Kev?' I asked. 'Because you'll have a bottle of wine under one arm, a box of chocolates under the other, a four-pack in one hand and my pressie in the other, won't you?' he replied. Yes, Sally, that's the kind of man you've married.

Have you noticed how few single people were invited here today? That was Kevin's idea as well. He's not stupid, despite rumours to the contrary. He told me that if he invited only married people all the presents would be clear profit. But in all honesty, Kevin doesn't know the meaning of the word meanness. Mind you he doesn't know the meaning of lots of other words either.

Talking of the meaning of words, do you know what the name Kevin actually means? Well, believe it or not, it comes from the Celtic word for handsome. Ridiculous isn't it? On the other hand, the name Sally means princess and who could argue with that?

When I asked Kevin about today's wedding arrangements, he said, 'Oh, I'll leave all that to you. But I do want Bells, and get at least a dozen bottles.' Well I don't know about Bells, but I work with Kevin at Fenn Street School and I can tell you he is one of the best Teachers I know.

Kevin, you are a very lucky man to have married Sally – but then again Sally, you are an equally lucky lady to have married Kevin, and on behalf of the bridesmaids, I wish you both love and happiness!

Now I believe there have been one or two tele-messages . . .

Model speech 42: Best man's reply

Formal reception – Example 2.

Ladies and Gentlemen, thank you, John, for those kind words about the bridesmaids. Personally, though, I would have gone even further. They are the most delightful set of bridesmaids I have ever seen. Be honest, today you are blinkered and you only have eyes for Janet – and who can blame you?

As Henry VIII said to each of his wives in turn, 'I shall not keep you long.' The reason for this is quite simple: I'm now supposed to sing the bridegroom's praises and tell you all about his good points. Unfortunately, I can't sing, and I can't think of any good points to tell you about – but I shall try.

What can I say about John that has not already been said in open court? There is nothing I wouldn't do for him and I know there is nothing he wouldn't do for me. In fact, we spend our lives doing nothing for each other.

But I must be very careful what I say about a dentist because one day I could find myself a captive audience in his chair, staring up at the ceiling – and I've seen *Marathon Man*. Last week I arranged to meet him after work at his surgery. I'd had trouble with the car and he said he'd take a look at it. I was a bit early so I glanced through the magazines and newspapers he provides for his patients in the waiting room. Wasn't it terrible about the *Titanic?* He did a great job on the car – but later it cost me £200 to have it overhauled. I was speeding down the M4 when a police car overhauled it.

That's one thing no one can accuse John of – speeding. Everything he does is calm and measured and he will never take any short-cuts. I remember at school we all had to count the traffic going past the main gate. Once Old Chalky – Mr White, our form teacher – had gone, we all went off and played soccer – all but John, of course, who spent the whole afternoon – yes, counting cars. The rest of us agreed we'd all report roughly the same number of cars, lorries and motor bikes to Old Chalky, so John got told off because all his answers were miles out from everybody else's.

But, looking back on it, that afternoon demonstrated how reliable and single-minded he is. It also shows he won't take the easy way out by going along with the crowd when he knows the crowd is wrong – or maybe it showed he doesn't like soccer. What it definitely did show was that he possessed something every aspiring dentist needs – patience, in both senses of the word. And today, John, your patience has been rewarded.

I can't understand why Janet chose you rather than me. But I suppose that it proves men have better taste than women. After all, John chose Janet, but Janet chose John. So now I come to my final wedding day duty which isn't a duty really – it's a real pleasure: on behalf of the bridesmaids and myself I sincerely wish you and your lovely wife, Janet, everlasting love and happiness!

Model speech 43: Best man's reply
Formal reception — Example 3.

Ladies and Gentlemen, I've been best man once before. I think it went OK last time – the couple in question are at least still talking to me. Unfortunately, they're not actually talking to each other. I thought Ruth knew Mark had slept with her younger sister before I mentioned it in my speech – but perhaps the fact he'd slept with her mother came as a surprise.

On such an illustrious day as this it seems odd for me to be called best man. After all, who pays attention to a man in my position today? They all say, 'Doesn't the bride look radiant?' – which she does, and 'What a charming set of bridesmaids' – which they are, and 'What a dashing bridegroom' – which he isn't. But who says, 'What a fine figure of a man the best man is' – which, so very obviously, he is. No, if they notice me at all, they think I'm a waiter or a chauffeur. One lady, who shall remain nameless, even asked if my name was Brad and had I been sent to meet her by the Lonely Hearts Club Escort Agency. But enough of my troubles.

When I made my other wedding speech a man fell asleep. I asked a pageboy to wake him and do you know what the little horror replied? He said, 'You wake him. You were the one who put him to sleep.' Well, today, to make sure I don't make the same mistake again, I promise to be brief.

You know, this really is a truly historic day! This day, the 21st of July, will always be associated with three of the great events of the last hundred years. Funnyman Robin Williams was born in 1952; Neil Armstrong took a giant leap for mankind in 1969; and on this day in 200X, William married Mary. So in 1969 it was Neil Armstrong, but today it is William who is over the moon.

We all know he likes a bit of a flutter and he told me he once dreamt he won eight million on the lottery. 'What would you do about all the begging letters if you ever did win that much?' I asked. 'Oh, I'd still keep sending them,' he replied. Well, today, William, you are not dreaming, and I can tell you you really have hit the jackpot. On behalf of the bridesmaids and myself I wish you both love and everlasting happiness!

Model speech 44: Best man's reply

Informal wedding party – Example 1.

Thank you for those kind words. The bridesmaids and I have really enjoyed this wonderful occasion. Layla said she wanted a simple wedding – and that's exactly what she got – starting with the groom. He is the most independent salesman I know – I can't remember the last time he took an order from anyone. He is also an avid book collector. Last week he complained to me that he had so many that he did not know what to do with them. I suggested he tried reading them. He must spend a lot of money on books, but I think things are going to change. As Layla walked up the aisle, and approached the altar, and sang a hymn, I heard her whisper to her dad, 'Aisle – altar – hymn.' Dougal, you have been warned. Now before I take a pew, on behalf of the bridesmaids, Layla and Dougal, I wish you peace and harmony!

Model speech 45: Best man's reply

Informal wedding party – Example 2.

On behalf of all the attendants, I'd like to thank you sincerely for those kind words. It has been a pleasure for us to have been a small part of your big day. They say that marriage is a process whereby the grocer acquires the account that used to be held by the florist. Well if that's true you won't find Reg complaining because, as you all know, Reg is a grocer. He tells me times are hard – you have to offer bargains to keep your customers. Have you seen the sign in his window? It says, 'Eggs still twelve a dozen.' What a bargain. Well, we're all delighted that Reg has decided to put all his eggs in one basket by marrying Maureen. He couldn't have made a better choice. And, as sure as eggs is eggs, they can look forward to – dare I say it? – an eggcellent future together. On behalf of the bridesmaids, Maureen and Reg, I wish you everlasting love and happiness!

Model speech 46: Chief bridesmaid's reply

Formal reception or informal wedding party – where the best man does not respond to the toast or, more unusually, where the chief bridesmaid does as well.

Thank you so much for those kind words. I know I also speak for my fellow bridesmaids when I say it has been a real pleasure for us all today. I have known Louise since she joined us at Blackwall eight years ago. Someone had told her to go to blazes so she decided to become a firefighter. I haven't known Alex for quite so long. He works for BR, but no one is perfect. I suppose he should have been the one carrying Louise's train today, not us. I told him I had to get home tonight and I asked him the time of the late train to London. 'Take the 10.15,' he suggested, 'that's usually as late as any.'

But enough of this banter. They say marriage is founded on mutual respect. If that is so then this marriage cannot fail. I know how much Alex respects Louise and Louise has told me her pet name for him, which could hardly be more respectful. She told me that as they sit before an open fire on a cold and damp February evening, and as yet another log is needed, she will turn lovingly to her beloved and say, 'Alexander – the grate'. Well, Alexander and Louise, we hope and pray that the future is great for you both and on behalf of myself and the other bridesmaids, I wish you everlasting love and happiness!

Model speech 47: Best man's reply

Formal reception or informal wedding party – where there are no bridesmaids, but there is a maid/matron of honour.

Thank you so much for those kind words. No one knows better than me how much the maid/matron of honour, Marlene, deserves your compliments and thanks. But for Marlene and me it has been a pleasure, not a duty, to have been a small part of your big day. We merely had the enjoyable tasks of assisting and helping to carry out the design and plan for this wedding so ably arranged by Kelly's parents, Frank and Kim. Not only that, they are such charming hosts and wonderful people that I am sure that everyone present here will want to stand and join Marlene and me in proposing a toast to Frank and Kim.

To Frank and Kim!

Model speech 48: Best man's reply

Formal reception or informal reception – where there are no bridesmaids.

Ladies and Gentlemen, the last time I made a wedding speech someone at the back shouted, 'I can't hear you!, – and a man sitting next to me yelled back, 'I'll change places with you!' [*pause*]. In order to avoid any possible musical chairs here today, I intend to speak up and then to shut up.

I have been a best man at many weddings and I admitted to Christopher that my track record has not been that brilliant:

'Could do better', as they used to write on our school reports. In my time I have lost the ring, gone to the wrong church and lost the honeymoon luggage. But did Chris care about these not-so-rare examples of maladministration? He did not. 'Don't worry,' he said, 'you won't have to do a thing. Just leave it all to Jayne's mum.' And he was right. Mildred, ably assisted by her husband George, really came up trumps. [*If possible, refer to some particularly outstanding feature, such as the beautiful flower arrangements or the magnificent buffet.*] They have created the perfect day – one we shall all remember. So I ask you to raise your glasses and to drink a toast to our friends – Jayne's parents and Christopher's new in-laws, George and Mildred.

To George and Mildred!

If there are no bridesmaids, the bridegroom may not require a speech by the best man (such as speeches 47 and 48). Instead, he might prefer this arrangement:

1. Toast to the couple by a close family friend or relative.

2. Response by the bridegroom.

3. Response by the bride's father.

The first speech could be similar to speech 2 or 15, according to whether you are at a formal reception or informal wedding party. The second could be similar to any of the speeches suitable for the bridegroom and the third similar to any of those suitable for the bride's father, although neither would propose a toast.

It is not uncommon for other guests to speak after the best man (or chief bridesmaid or bridesmaid's father). However, the danger is that too many people will try to get on the bandwagon, especially after the fire water has flowed liberally. If there are to be any speeches after the reply on behalf of the bridesmaids, it is best to keep other contributions to a minimum, possibly as follows:

1. Toast to the hosts by a close friend or relative of the bridegroom.

2. Reply by the bride's father.

3. The best man reads the tele-messages.

Model speech 49: Close friend or relative of bridegroom's toast of thanks to the host and hostess

Ladies and Gentlemen, what a wonderful day this has been. Everything has run so smoothly from the word go. And who do we have to thank for that? Steve was such a fine and efficient best man and the bridesmaids added so much to the occasion. But our greatest thanks must go to our hosts, Christina's parents and Paul's new in-laws, Margaret and Denis. After all, they organised this event and frankly I don't think it could have been bettered. [*If possible, mention some particularly outstanding aspect of the day – food, music, dancing or whatever.*] I am sure everyone present will want to stand and join me as I propose a toast to our magnificent hosts, Margaret and Denis.

Ladies and Gentlemen, Margaret and Denis!

Model speech 50: Bride's father's reply to the toast

A longer reply, similar to one of speeches 1–21, but without the toast, is acceptable if he has not spoken before.

Thank you, Nigel, for those most generous words. I'm only going to speak for a moment or two because of my throat – if I go on any longer than that Margaret has threatened to cut it. Of course, it was an absolute pleasure for us to do our bit to help make the day the success it has so clearly been. But the greatest credit must go to you all for making it such a joyous occasion. You have been fantastic. And I hope you will all continue to have a wonderful time this afternoon/evening!

Further Reading

WEDDINGS – GENERAL

The Good Wedding Guide, Sue Carpenter (Equation).
Getting Married, Sarah Caisley (Mason).
Getting Married, Mary Gostelow (Batsford).
The Bridal Path, Eve Anderson (Foulsham).
The Complete Wedding Book, Jill Thomas (World's Work).
The Wedding Day Book, Sue Dobson (Arrow).

PLANNING A WEDDING

Planning a Wedding, Mary Kilborn (How To Books).
Planning Your Wedding, Joyce Robins (Hamlyn).
The Step-by-Step Wedding Planner, Eve Anderson (Foulsham).
The Wedding Planner, Angela Lansbury (Ward Lock).
The Complete Wedding Planner, Gail Lawther (Harper Collins).

WEDDING ETIQUETTE

Wedding Etiquette, Patricia and William Derraugh (Foulsham).

Wedding Etiquette, Angela Lansbury (Ward Lock).

Wedding Etiquette Properly Explained, Vernon Heaton (Elliot Right Way Books).

The Complete Guide to Wedding Etiquette, Margot Lawrence (Ward Lock).

THE MAIN PLAYERS

The Bride's Book, Drusilla Beyfus (Allen Lane).

The Bridegroom's Handbook, Sean Callery (Ward Lock).

Making the Bridegroom's Speech, John Bowden (How To Books).

The Best Man's Handbook, Henry Russell (David and Charles).

How to be the Best Man, Angela Lansbury (Ward Lock).

Making the Best Man's Speech, John Bowden (How To Books).

The Complete Best Man, John Bowden (How To Books)

Making the Father of the Bride's Speech, John Bowden (How To Books).

The Complete Father of the Bride, John Bowden (How To Books).

How to be a Bridesmaid, Angela Lansbury (Ward Lock).

SECOND WEDDINGS

Emily Post on Second Weddings, Emily Post (Harper Perennial).

PUBLIC SPEAKING

Mitch Murray's Handbook for the Terrified Speaker, (Foulsham).

Just Say A Few Words, Bob Monkhouse (Lennard Publishing).

Mastering Public Speaking, Anne Nicholls (How To Books).

The Complete Public Speaker, Gyles Brandreth (Robert Hale).

Janner's Complete Speechmaker, Greville Janner (Business Books).

Debrett's Guide to Speaking in Public, Carole McKenzie (Headline).

Powerful Business Speeches, John Bowden (How To Books).

Speaking in Public, John Bowden (How To Books).

ANNIVERSARIES

Today's the Day, Jeremy Beadle (W.H. Allen).

The Amazing Almanac, Gyles Brandreth (Pelham Books).

The Book of Days, Anthony Frewin (Collins).

The Anniversary Book, Christopher Downing (Futura).

Hamlyn Dictionary of Dates and Anniversaries (Hamlyn).

Chambers' Dates (Chambers).

On This Day: The History of the World in 366 Days, Sian Facer, Editor (Hamlyn).

QUOTATIONS

The library shelves are weighed down with these books. I find the following particularly useful:

The Oxford Book of Quotations (OUP).

Stevenson's Book of Quotations (Cassell).

The Penguin Dictionary of Humorous Quotations, Fred Metcalf (Viking).

Cassell's Book of Humorous Quotations (Cassell).

The New Penguin Dictionary of Quotations (Viking).

A Dictionary of Twentieth Century Quotations, Nigel Rees (Fontana).

The Guinness Dictionary of Quotations for all Occasions, Gareth Sharpe (Guinness Publishing).

A Dictionary of Contemporary Quotations (David and Charles).

The Oxford Dictionary of Modern Quotations (OUP).

Apt and Amusing Quotations, G.F. Lamb (Elliot Right Way Books).

ANECDOTES AND JOKES

There are hundreds – perhaps thousands – of these books. Here is a personal selection:

One Liners for Weddings, Mitch Murray (Foulsham).

The Faber Book of Anecdotes, Clifton Fadiman (Faber).

Jokes and Quotes for Speeches, Peter Eldin (Ward Lock).

The Right Joke for the Right Occasion, Kevin Goldstein-Jackson (Elliot Right Way Books).

1497 Jokes, Stories and Anecdotes, Herbert V. Prochnow (Sterling).

3500 Good Jokes for Speakers, Gerald Lieberman (Thorsons).

5000 One- and Two-Line Jokes, Leopold Fechter (Thorsons).

The Penguin Dictionary of Jokes, Fred Metcalf (Viking).

MISCELLANEOUS

The Power of Your Subconscious Mind, Joseph Murphy (Simon and Schuster).

Use Your Head, Tony Buzan (BBC/Open University).

Voice and the Actor, Cicely Berry (Virgin).

Body Language, Michael Pease (Positive Paperbacks).

Simple Relaxation, Laura Mitchell (John Murray).

Visualisation, Ursula Markham (Element Books).

Index